Breakeven Analysis

Breakeven Analysis

The Definitive Guide to Cost-Volume-Profit Analysis

Second Edition

Michael E. Cafferky and Jon Wentworth

 BUSINESS EXPERT PRESS

Breakeven Analysis: The Definitive Guide to Cost-Volume-Profit Analysis,
Second Edition
Copyright © Business Expert Press, LLC, 2014.

First published in 2010 by
Business Expert Press, LLC
222 East 46th Street, New York, NY 10017
www.businessexpertpress.com

ISBN-13: 978-1-63157-091-9 (paperback)
ISBN-13: 978-1-63157-092-6 (e-book)

Business Expert Press Managerial Accounting Collection

Collection ISSN: 2152-7113 (print)
Collection ISSN: 2152-7121 (electronic)

Cover and interior design by Exeter Premedia Services Private Ltd, Chennai, India

First edition: 2010
Second edition: 2014

10 9 8 7 6 5 4 3 2 1

Printed in the United States of America.

Abstract

This book is a comprehensive collection of cost-volume-profit applications. Business professionals, entrepreneurs, business professors, and undergraduate and graduate business students will benefit from this one-stop how-to book of formulas, explanations, and examples. The user will find a wide range of topics, from calculating basic breakeven, to dealing with multiple products, mixed costs, changing costs, and changing prices.

Keywords

Annuity factor, breakeven (BE), cash flow, coefficient of determination, common stock dividend (CD), common stockholders, contribution margin (CM), contribution margin ratio, cost of capital, cost of goods sold (COGS), cost-volume-profit (CVP) analysis, demand, fixed costs (FC), high-low method, income statement, income tax, least squares method, multiple regression, net present value (NPV), operating leverage, polynomial, preferred stock dividend (PD), preferred stockholders, price elasticity of demand, quadratic formula, scattergraph, target profit, total cost, total revenue, unit selling price (SP), unit variable costs (VC), weighted average contribution margin, weighted average selling price

Contents

Preface

Seldom does a manager go more than a month or two without employing the thinking patterns that are at the foundation of this book. In some rapidly changing organizations, breakeven calculations will be used as fodder for discussions, debates, and ultimately decisions on a daily or weekly basis.

Today's managers are far more sophisticated than those of a generation ago, but the need for cost-volume-profit thinking and breakeven decision-making tools has not gone away. Advances in cost accounting; the use of activity-based costing; the use of many performance-improvement tools such as identifying and removing constraints, optimizing logistics, and inventory management all lead down two interrelated pathways: value improvement and cost reduction.

Many existing companies have already picked the low-hanging fruit of performance improvement. With each passing year the gains from squeezing costs out of current systems become more and more difficult to achieve. These efforts have an impact on the breakeven point of the organization. New companies, their managers learning fast from competitors, begin with the need to know where the breakeven point is. Breakeven thinking becomes second nature to seasoned managers who are faced with the ever-present need to fend off the onslaughts of competitors who are finding more efficient ways of doing business.

Who This Book Is Designed For

We start with the assumption that the users of this book will vary in their degrees of sophistication in terms of cost-volume-profit analysis. Some readers will have no business school background but have worked their way up to middle or senior management learning business concepts primarily in the context of their organization and industry. We take these readers from the basic concepts up through the advanced approaches. Some of these managers work in nonprofit organizations and government agencies, which may not be attempting to achieve a profit but are nevertheless concerned about the prosperity of their organization. Many of these readers will have had no formal training in managerial accounting. We believe they will benefit from seeing this collection of tools. Practice and use of these tools will contribute toward these managers becoming more useful to their organizations.

Another group of users is entrepreneurs who, if they have been successful, have learned about breakeven thinking and analysis from their own experience. Many entrepreneurs don't go to business school, preferring to learn from their experiences in the market. This simple tool kit can bring into clear understanding much of what these entrepreneurs have been thinking about for a long time but didn't have the range of tools readily available to do what they know needs to be done. As their enterprises grow and become more complex, they face the prospect of helping their top-level and midlevel management teams improve their thinking about the business. When dealing with suppliers and customers, many of these entrepreneurs will improve their negotiating abilities by incorporating breakeven analysis into the negotiation process. Understanding the breakeven point of your supplier and your customer can be just as valuable as knowing your own company's breakeven point. In many negotiating situations the simple but effective tools discussed here provide insight and clarity, which can, if effectively presented, cut through the smoke and mirrors to the truth, revealing flaws or strengths in particular arguments.

Other users will have completed undergraduate business school and followed a career track that finds them in managerial positions. Most of these readers were exposed to one or two of the tools we present here. Still other readers will be MBA graduates who are at or heading toward senior-level leadership positions. Depending on the degree program they completed, they were exposed to one or more breakeven analysis tools in graduate school.

The last group of users will be undergraduate and graduate business students whose professors see value in exposing them to more than just one or two methods to calculate breakeven.

The Plan of the Book

Think of this book as a ready-to-use managerial tool kit, which if used frequently will sharpen the manager's ability to make decisions. We explain the vocabulary of breakeven analysis, also known as cost-volume-profit (CVP) analysis, explore the breadth of applications of CVP, and illustrate the use of CVP concepts in a broad range of management and marketing scenarios. While this book is not a comprehensive treatment of the topic, we employ many examples from several different types of industries to illustrate breakeven calculations.

The user of this book will find here a wide range of interrelated tools, from how to calculate basic breakeven to dealing with multiple products, mixed costs, changing conditions, and conditions of uncertainty. After an introductory chapter we present several commonly used breakeven analysis tools. With each tool we present one or more examples showing how the calculations work and the types of information needed for each one.

We hope this collection of practical tools will add value to your work as a manager regardless of where in the world of commerce, nonprofit, and government organizations you serve others.

Michael E. Cafferky and Jon Wentworth
Southern Adventist University
Collegedale, Tennessee

CHAPTER 1

Introduction

Since its introduction in the 19th century, the breakeven concept has been used, enhanced, adjusted, and extended in an attempt to reduce or correct for its limitations and make it applicable to more and more business situations. In spite of its limitations and criticisms, detailed in Appendix B, breakeven analysis (also known as cost-volume-profit analysis) continues to be one of the best ways to focus on the relationship between cost, volume, and profitability. We present here the applications and approaches that we believe managers will find most useful.

The Essence of Breakeven Analysis

Cost-volume-profit analysis is not just the mathematical result generated by applying a particular math formula. It is not merely a single number used at a point in time, such as the number of units of a company's products that it needs to produce and sell. In essence breakeven analysis is *a continual way of thinking* used by people potentially everywhere in the organization as they deal with a variety of decisions. As such it embraces the common ground of thinking that is used in accounting and economics.[1]

Overall breakeven thinking is *a way of comparing the amount of incoming value that an organization needs in order to serve its customers by delivering outgoing value of an equal amount.* When applied to specific situations that might be changing, breakeven thinking is a way of comparing the impact of an anticipated change with the current situation. When these values can be quantified, a breakeven formula may be applied. But when values are intangible or unquantifiable, a mental comparison is still made.

The Traditional Breakeven Formula

Traditionally, breakeven has been expressed in one of two ways. If the desired result is the quantity of units that must be sold to achieve breakeven, the following formula is used:

$$\frac{\text{Fixed Costs}}{\text{Contribution Margin per Unit}} = \text{Breakeven in Units to Be Sold} = BE_U$$

If, however, the desired result is the dollar amount of sales required to reach breakeven, the following formula is used:

$$\frac{\text{Fixed Costs}}{\text{Contribution Margin Ratio per Unit}} = \text{Breakeven in Dollars to Be Sold} = BE_\$$$

Business Situations Where Breakeven Analysis Is Useful

You will find in various accounting textbooks the traditional simple formula for calculating breakeven for a company that produces and sells a single product. Some texts offer breakeven formulas for multiple-product companies. The simplicity of these formulas has opened breakeven analysis to criticisms. The following list illustrates some of the ways in which breakeven thinking and breakeven analysis can be used:

- Deciding whether to quit your job and start new company
- Deciding whether to outsource
- Deciding whether to change capacity
- Evaluating customer profitability
- Making capital budget decisions
- Deciding whether to start selling products on the Internet
- Making changes to pricing policies
- Evaluating how best to monitor operations on a daily, weekly, or monthly basis
- Calculating the impact of changing prices and costs
- Developing sales incentive programs

- Determining the minimum number of transactions to complete per day, per week, or per month
- Deciding to modify the composition of a product

Expressing breakeven thinking in terms of *value* will naturally lead us to consider the tangible, explicit values measured by cost and revenue. To this we turn next.

CHAPTER 2

Total Cost Method

In this chapter we introduce the fundamental calculation that defines cost-volume-profit analysis from an accounting perspective. Let's start with a short story.

Three managers at a manufacturing firm, Sharon Elsworth, Dante Jackson, and Larry Meeks, were having lunch together. After a couple of minutes of small talk, Dante said to the others, "Have you noticed that consumer demand is going through the roof for our product? Keep in mind that this is just a single-stage model. What no one is making, however, is a two-stage model. Haven't you thought about that? I think about this so much I sometimes can't get to sleep at night. It's only a matter of time before someone will come out with the two-stager."

Sharon said, "I've been so busy getting the bills paid and producing financial statements that I haven't thought about a lot of things lately!"

Dante said, "I already talked with the big boss about this. He rejected the idea, saying that we need to stay with what we do best and ramp up our economies of scale more because there will come a day when the price will drop and we need to be prepared to weather the storm of heavier price competition. What do you think about the idea of us three working together, getting some investors together, and starting another production company?"

Larry said, "You've got to be kidding!"

Dante replied, "I'm sure we could get approval from the board to start another company. We wouldn't have to quit our jobs right now. True, making a two-stager would be a little different from the model that is on the market now. But we know the basic operational side of this business. Think of the money we could make right now!"

The group began brainstorming and kicking around some numbers. Larry grabbed one of the paper napkins from the table and began jotting down figures. From the questions that surfaced around the table, we can see that their minds were starting to evaluate the fundamental elements of a business model.

Sharon asked, "Do you really think this would work? What I want to know is how we will be able to pay our bills."

Larry asked, "What will it take to make a profit? I don't want to get into this unless there is an opportunity to make some money!"

Dante said, "True, we need to know that we will be able to get to breakeven, otherwise it won't be worth it. We know the market price on the current model. If we made a two-stage model, it would sell at a price premium since it would offer more flexibility to users. At 500,000 units, which is just 5% of the demand of the current model, and a price that is 40% higher than the price point on the current model, pay attention! We are talking $10 million of total annual revenue here folks—$10 million!" He wrote this figure in large characters on the napkin.

Larry said, "True, but the costs of producing a two-stager would be higher, too. How do we know that we will be able to make this two-stage model, pay for the cost of running the business, and still break even?

Sharon reminded them, "What you are saying, Dante, is that we will be able to operate the business including the management, engineering, production, and a dynamite marketing team, and still pay for all the materials, packing, and other stuff for no more than $10 million. That is pretty aggressive given what we know about the production and marketing costs of the current model! I'd like to know what it would cost to make just one of these two-stagers, let alone 500,000 of them!"

What Sharon, Dante, and Larry are talking about is the first and most fundamental application of breakeven thinking.

One of the fundamental ways to apply breakeven analysis is by simply thinking about the point where total revenue equals total costs for a defined period of time.[1] This is one definition of the breakeven point.

Using the distinction between fixed costs (FC) and variable costs (VC), we can also say that we have reached the breakeven point when total revenue equals the sum of fixed costs and variable costs.

The Formula

Total Costs for Period = Total Revenue for Period = Breakeven

or

(Fixed Costs + Variable Costs) = Total Revenue = Breakeven.

Since total revenue equals the quantity sold times the unit selling price, we can also extend this breakeven cost-to-revenue relationship with the following formula:

(Fixed Costs + Variable Costs) =
(Quantity Sold × Unit Selling Price) = Breakeven.

Example 1

The owner of Attashay Company develops the following data table for a specific period:

Fixed Costs = $520,000

Variable Costs = $1,105,000

Total Costs = $1,625,000

The scale of costs represented here is different from that of many businesses. To make this and other examples in this book align with the scale of operation in your situation, simply append to or remove zeros from the total.

The following would be Attashay Company's breakeven point for the period:

($520,000 + $1,105,000) Total Costs =
$1,625,000 Total Revenue = Breakeven.

Interpreting the Result

The breakeven amount is the dollar amount for the period that is spent on operating expenses or generated in sales revenue. If you estimate the total costs, you know what your total revenue must be and vice versa.

Users of this information will focus on one or the other side of the equation. For example, the accountant may be more interested in the total cost side, knowing the history or the expected future of revenue generation. The marketing leader may likely be focused on the total revenue side of the equation as he or she thinks about the sales and marketing processes needed to cover expected costs.

Notice that although dollars are used to calculate the breakeven point, it is at this point that whatever number of units that have been produced and sold also is the breakeven in terms of units.

Depending on the type of business and the frequency with which this type of analysis helps in decision making, the relevant time period can be any common unit such as daily, weekly, monthly, quarterly, or annually. Annual total cost estimates can be broken down on a monthly basis and adjusted for known fluctuations in costs. Just recognize that as the time period increases in length, the presence of other influences on the change in costs and revenue will become greater.

This application of breakeven analysis looks at the business model's big picture. It represents the overall magnitude of operations. Such an overview can be helpful when only generalized results are needed, and changes to the structure of fixed costs and variable costs are believed to be minimal. This broad-stroke approach can be useful as an initial approximating method when details are not available. The big-picture approach also is less costly in terms of time and effort. However, since it takes such a broad view, it leaves undefined important details that, if known, could improve the precision of the breakeven calculation. One can think of this approach as yielding the crudest results.[2]

For some business situations, details on costs, revenue, or pricing may be difficult to obtain, such as in the early stages of planning for a new venture. The broad approach taken by this basic formula leaves out consideration of the number of units of the product or service that need to be produced and sold during the time period. It says nothing about the sales mix. Precise estimates of total costs and total revenue for a business operation may be difficult to determine in advance. Differentiating between fixed and variable costs may also be difficult.

Extending the Formula

For some situations, if the company sells one product and if an estimate of the going market price for that product is known and the decision maker assumes that the company needs to match this market price, this information can be used to estimate the number of units the company needs to produce. The following example shows this calculation:

$$\text{Total Costs} = \text{Quantity Sold} \times \text{Unit Selling Price} = \text{Breakeven}$$

$$\frac{\text{Total Costs}}{\text{Unit Selling Price}} = \text{Quantity Sold to Break Even}$$

So, for example, in Attashay Company if

$$\text{Total Costs} = \$1{,}625{,}000$$

$$\text{Unit Selling Price (Market Price)} = \$25$$

then the breakeven point is

$$\frac{\$1{,}625{,}000 \text{ Total Costs}}{\$25 \text{ Unit Selling Price}} = 465{,}000 \text{ Units Sold to Break Even.}$$

Using an estimate of the market price conveys an important economic assumption for the use of this formula for decision making. Company managers are assuming that if the market price must be used in order to be competitive, then customers will be highly responsive to changes in price. The company and its competitors, under this situation, are left with the prospect of competing not only on price but also correspondingly on their relative abilities to lower their respective cost structures if they expect to continue earning a profit.

Linking operational activities with the breakeven formula is vital if you want to get the most value out of breakeven thinking. As we will see in later chapters of this book, to be practical on a day-to-day basis the breakeven amount expressed in either dollars or units must be converted into a percentage of operational capacity. In the example given previously, if company managers estimate that they will need to produce and sell 465,000 units to break even, they must begin asking themselves some serious questions, including the following:

- What is estimated capacity given our current cost structure?
- What percentage of capacity must we use in order to achieve the breakeven amount?
- What kinds and amounts of hardware technologies will be needed in order to provide the capacity required to break even?
- Given a certain number of workdays per month, how many units must be produced monthly? Weekly? Daily?
- What configurations of employees, equipment, and other resources will be needed on a daily basis to achieve breakeven?
- If we are constrained by fixed capacity, what additional fixed costs will be incurred to bring capacity up to a level where we can break even? How will these additional fixed costs change the breakeven point?
- What level of intensity must sales and marketing activities employ in order to stimulate demand sufficient to break even?

Think of the total cost method as the first opportunity to test your assumptions about the market and about your company's ability to meet market needs. To the degree that your assumptions are accurate, the big picture of your company's business model will be an accurate reflection of what the company and every department in it needs to do daily.

Additional Application

This basic formula uses summary data from an income statement. But the same principle can be applied when using data from the statement of cash flows as follows:

Total Cash In = Total Cash Out = Breakeven Point for Period.

This formula can be applied to a portion of the statement of cash flows, such as just the cash flows from operations or just the cash flows from investments.

The extension of this basic formula leads us naturally to think about the other approaches to breakeven analysis. To these we turn next.

CHAPTER 3

Contribution Margin Method

The basic approach to the breakeven calculation is the contribution margin method. This method is a refinement of the total cost method. This method, which indicates the number of units that must be produced and sold, is particularly useful to people involved in the acquisition of raw material and labor, actual production of the finished product, and storage and shipping of the product. The resulting target value of units to be produced and sold will guide many of the departmental functions of a company. The number of units required to meet the target focuses the production side of the company on how much work must be done. The purchasing department will base materials purchases on "the number." Human resources will decide how many employees are needed; the production manager will decide how to schedule production runs and work shifts; the warehouse manager will gauge how much storage space is needed; and the transportation department will arrange for adequate containers, trucks and trailers, or rail cars to handle the volume of goods to be shipped.

To apply this method, the user needs to know the selling price per unit, the variable cost per unit, and the total fixed costs for the period being analyzed. Contribution margin (CM) is the difference between revenues and variable costs. Recall that the contribution margin is calculated as the selling price per unit less the variable cost per unit. The contribution margin tells you that after the variable costs have been covered, each unit of product or service sold to the customer contributes a certain amount toward paying for fixed costs.

The contribution margin method expresses breakeven as

$$\frac{\text{Fixed Costs}}{\text{Contribution Margin per Unit}} = \text{Breakeven in Units to Be Sold.}$$

Let's use the following data for an example:

$$\text{Annual Fixed Costs} = \$520,000$$

$$\text{Selling Price per Unit} = \$25$$

$$\text{Variable Cost per Unit} = \$17$$

$$\text{Contribution Margin per Unit} = (\$25 - \$17) = \$8$$

The following is this company's breakeven point:

$$\frac{\$520,000 \text{ Annual Fixed Costs}}{\$8 \text{ CM per Unit}} = 65,000 \text{ Units to Be Sold Annually.}$$

Interpreting the Result

The breakeven number is the quantity of units that must be sold in the time allowed by the fixed costs incurred. The time period may be a day, a week, a month, a year, or any other period of time. Our example company may wish to think in terms of breakeven each week. In that case, we could divide the annual fixed costs by 52 weeks and recalculate the breakeven point:

$$\frac{\$10,000 \text{ Weekly Fixed Costs}}{\$8 \text{ CM per Unit}} = 1,250 \text{ Units to Be Sold Each Week.}$$

Recall that one way to understand the breakeven point is the point where net income equals zero. With this breakeven information, we can confirm that our calculations are correct using Table 3.1.

With this information expressed in terms of weekly units, company managers will naturally think about the production processes, inventory

Table 3.1. Breakeven Income Statement

Weekly sales (1,250 units sold at $25 per unit)	$31,250
Variable costs (1,250 units at $17 per unit)	$21,250
Contribution margin (the difference between weekly sales revenue and weekly variable costs)	$10,000
Weekly fixed costs	$10,000
Net income (the difference between contribution margin and fixed costs)	$0

management, support equipment, and other resources that need to be in place and used consistently. Support departments will be organized around the production departments, which are organized around the production goals. Sales and marketing personnel will begin thinking about the kinds of activities needed to stimulate demand. Managers will take into consideration any seasonality to patterns of demand. Financial managers will think about the amount of working capital (cash) needed to support the operations.

Extending the Formula: The Contribution Margin Ratio Method

As stated previously, certain users need information stated in units. Other users are "top line" driven and need to know the breakeven point in sales dollars instead of units to be sold. The sales dollars necessary to meet the target focuses the marketing side of the company on how much work must be done. These users would plan how many contacts must be made with prospective customers, how many deals must be closed or transactions completed, how many sales representatives must be hired to make those contacts, the sales travel-expense budget, the type and quantity of promotional efforts, and the budget for sales commissions for the coming year.

One advantage of the contribution margin ratio method over the basic contribution margin method is that the ratio method can be applied whether the number of units is known or unknown, since the ratio can be obtained from per unit amounts or from total amounts.

If the breakeven point in units is already known, then the breakeven point in sales dollars would be calculated as selling price per unit times breakeven sales units. Continuing with the annual data from the preceding example, the breakeven point in sales dollars would be

65,000 Units to Be Sold × $25 Selling Price per Unit = $1,625,000.

If the breakeven point in units is not already known, then the breakeven point in sales dollars could be calculated directly:

$$\frac{\text{Fixed Costs}}{\text{Contribution Margin Ratio}} = \text{Breakeven in Sales Dollars}$$

The contribution margin ratio (CM ratio) expressed as a percentage is calculated:

$$\frac{\text{Contribution Margin per Unit}}{\text{Selling Price per Unit}} = \text{CM Ratio.}$$

Applying our previous per unit data, the CM ratio would be

$$\frac{\$8 \text{ CM per Unit}}{\$25 \text{ Selling Price per Unit}} = 0.32 \text{ or } 32\%.$$

The CM ratio may also be calculated:

$$\frac{\text{Total Contribution Margin}}{\text{Total Revenue}} = \text{CM Ratio.}$$

For illustration's sake, let's assume the company sells 70,000 units annually. Applying our previous data using total amounts, the contribution margin would be

$$\frac{\text{Total CM (\$8 per Unit} \times 70,000 \text{ Units)}}{\text{Total Revenue (\$25} \times 70,000 \text{ Units)}} = 32\% \text{ CM Ratio.}$$

The choice between calculating the contribution margin ratio with per unit amounts and calculating the ratio with total amounts depends on the data available to the user.

Recall that the annual fixed costs were $520,000. So the breakeven in sales dollars would be

$$\frac{\$520,000 \text{ Annual Fixed Costs}}{0.32 \text{ CM Ratio}} = \$1,625,000 \text{ to Be Sold Annually.}$$

The CM ratio method can be applied to various time periods (weekly, monthly, or quarterly, for example), just as with the CM method. Let's see how much the sales budget must be for one week, using our previous weekly data.

$$\frac{\$10,000 \text{ Weekly Fixed Costs}}{0.32 \text{ CM Ratio}} = \$31,250 \text{ to Be Sold Each Week.}$$

We can check that sales target by multiplying the breakeven sales units by the unit selling price:

1,250 Units × $25 Selling Price per Unit = $31,250.

In alternate settings, the contribution margin may be calculated on a product line, a division producing multiple products, a customer, or a sales region.

A Few Notes on Operating Leverage

While the subject of operating leverage deserves more attention than we can give it in a book focused just on breakeven analysis, a few notes are appropriate.

Something interesting to observe with the contribution margin method is the effect on the breakeven point of fixed costs and of variable costs. As fixed costs increase, the breakeven point increases and the profit potential of the organization goes up with increased volume of sales. But if the sales level (demand) drops, the company will have difficulty in paying its fixed costs and the loss potential also goes up. For companies that face an uncertain or widely fluctuating demand, keeping fixed costs low minimizes the risks that come with fixed costs. This is one reason we see entrepreneurs keeping the fixed costs of their businesses low until they get established. As unit variable costs increase, the breakeven point increases and of course the profit potential goes down. As the ratio of fixed costs to variable costs increases, we say that the company's operating leverage increases since a small percent change in sales will lead to a large percent change in operating profit. The formula that is usually employed to calculate operating leverage is as follows:

Operating Leverage = % Change in Earnings Before Interest and Taxes ÷ % Change in Sales.

The following is the shorthand version of the formula:

$$OL = \%\zeta EBIT \div \%\Delta Sales,$$

where

$\%\Delta EBIT$ = % Change in Earnings Before Interest and Taxes

$\%\Delta Sales$ = Percent Change in Sales.

Organizations have varying degrees of choice regarding the amount of fixed costs and the amount of variable costs to incur. For example, a company in one industry may have the option of purchasing a new piece of equipment that will improve the efficiency of production (lower the variable costs per unit) while at the same time increasing fixed costs such as paying for routine maintenance or utility costs. A company in another industry, because of the nature of the business, may not have this flexibility. Companies that offer services typically have very high fixed costs and low variable costs. The attractiveness of the profits from services entices entrepreneurs to start service businesses, but the volatility of sales can make new service businesses more risky because of the high fixed costs.

The concept of contribution margin is helpful in many applications of breakeven thinking. We will consider some of these starting with the next chapter: calculating breakeven to achieve a target profit.

CHAPTER 4

Target Profit Method

While knowing the breakeven point is useful information, the objective of every business is to go beyond breakeven and achieve a profit. We can incorporate the target profit of the business into the breakeven formula in one of two ways.

Management may set a fixed amount of desired profit for the period (month, quarter, or year). That fixed desired profit is treated as an additional fixed cost in the formula.

$$\frac{\text{Fixed Costs + Desired Profit}}{\text{Contribution Margin (CM) per Unit}} = \frac{\text{Units to Be Sold to}}{\text{Achieve Desired Profit}}$$

Let's continue using the data from the example in the preceding chapter and add a desired profit of $52,000 per year.

Annual Fixed Costs = $520,000

Selling Price per Unit = $25

Variable Cost per Unit = $17

Contribution Margin per Unit = $8

Annual Desired Profit = $52,000

Including the desired profit in the equation, the breakeven point is as follows:

$$\frac{\$520,000 \text{ Annual Fixed Costs +}\$52,000 \text{ Desired Profit}}{\$8 \text{ Contribution Margin per Unit}} = \frac{71,500 \text{ Units to Be}}{\text{Sold Annually.}}$$

If management wants to set a weekly sales target, the calculation would be

$$\frac{\$10{,}000 \text{ Weekly Fixed Costs} + \$1{,}000}{\$8 \text{ Contribution Margin per Unit}} = \frac{137.5 \text{ Units to Be}}{\text{Sold Each Week.}}$$

While mathematically correct, our solution for the weekly sales target presents a problem. Customers generally buy complete products, not fractional portions of products. To resolve this problem, simply round any fractional unit up to the next higher whole unit. Our sales target per week would be 138 units.

As with the basic breakeven calculation, we can calculate the sales dollars required to reach the desired profit:

$$\frac{\$520{,}000 \text{ Annual Fixed Costs} + \$52{,}000 \text{ Desired Profit}}{0.32 \text{ CM Ratio } (\$8 \div \$25)} = \frac{\$1{,}787{,}500 \text{ to be}}{\text{Sold Annually}}$$

or

71,500 Units Sold Annually × $25 Selling Price per Unit = $1,787,500 Annual Sales.

Alternatively, management might express its profit objective as an amount per unit of sales, a variable target profit. The formula would be modified this way:

$$\frac{\text{Fixed Costs}}{\text{Contribution Margin per Unit} - \text{Desired Profit per Unit}} = \frac{\text{Units to Be Sold to}}{\text{Achieve Desired Profit.}}$$

Here again are our data:

Annual Fixed Costs = $520,000

Selling Price per Unit = $25

Variable Cost per Unit = $17

Contribution Margin per Unit = $8

Desired Profit per Unit = $2

$$\frac{\$520{,}000 \text{ Annual Fixed Costs}}{\$8 \text{ CM per Unit} - \$2 \text{ Desired Profit per Unit}} = \begin{array}{l} 86{,}666.67 \text{ Units to Be} \\ \text{Sold Annually.} \end{array}$$

And, as before, the fractional unit would be rounded up, so the sales target is 86,667 units.

If management wanted to see the weekly sales target in units, we would calculate it like this:

$$\frac{\$10{,}000 \text{ Weekly Fixed Costs}}{\$8 \text{ CM per Unit} - \$2 \text{ Desired Profit per Unit}} = \begin{array}{l} 1{,}666.67 \text{ Units to Be} \\ \text{Sold Each Week.} \end{array}$$

This rounds up to 1,667 units sold per week.

Again, the sales dollars required to achieve the target profit can be calculated. First, we need to recalculate the contribution margin ratio: $\$6 \div \$25 = 0.24$ or 24%.

Then calculate the annual sales dollars needed:

$$\frac{\$520{,}000 \text{ Annual Fixed Costs}}{0.24 \text{ CM Ratio}} = \begin{array}{l} \$2{,}166{,}667 \text{ (rounded)} \\ \text{to Be Sold Annually.} \end{array}$$

A refined approach to applying the target profit method was suggested by Bell.[1] Instead of using a single value for desired profit, he suggested that preferred stock and common stock dividends be added to the fixed costs. Under this approach, our formula would be

$$\frac{\begin{array}{c} \text{Fixed Costs + Preferred Stock Divi-} \\ \text{dend + Common Stock Dividend +} \\ \text{Desired Profit} \end{array}}{\text{Contribution Margin per Unit}} = \text{Breakeven.}$$

Using the data from the beginning of this chapter and adding dividend information, the calculation works out like this:

Annual Fixed Costs (FC) = $520,000

Selling Price per Unit = $25

Variable Cost per Unit = $17

Contribution Margin per Unit (CM) = $8

Annual desired profit to be retained by the company (RE) = $52,000

Dividends to be paid to preferred stockholders (PD) = $13,000

Dividends to be paid to common stockholders (CD) = $20,000

$$\frac{\$520{,}000 \text{ FC} + \$52{,}000 \text{ RE} + \$13{,}000 \text{ PD} + \$20{,}000 \text{ CD}}{\$8 \text{ CM per Unit}} = \begin{array}{l} 75{,}625 \text{ Units to Be} \\ \text{Sold Annually.} \end{array}$$

Ideally, contribution margin is identified using selling price and variable costs. When variable cost data are difficult to get, we need an alternative approach. The cost of goods sold method is one such approach, to which we turn next.

CHAPTER 5

Cost of Goods Sold Method

In situations where the volume of different products makes the traditional approach impractical, the cost of goods sold (COGS) method[1] may be more appropriate. For example, you operate a restaurant that offers a large number of menu selections to customers. Calculating the unit variable cost for each menu item might be difficult when many ingredients are used in small amounts for each item sold. The selling price of each menu item is known, but the combination of menu items that each customer selects is highly variable, making the job of calculating the unit selling price very difficult. Over time we may be able to develop some rules of thumb for average per-customer revenue for different times of day and different seasons of the year. Using averages will likely reduce the precision of our estimate. Thus, calculating the breakeven point for each menu item would likely be impractical.

The Formula

The basic breakeven relationships still apply, such as the fact that your restaurant incurs fixed costs and there is a potential for each meal served to provide a contribution margin (CM) toward covering fixed costs.

Breakeven (in dollars) = Fixed Costs ÷ Contribution Margin %

The first task is to identify which of the expense items on the income statement represent fixed costs. The next step is to identify the contribution margin.

Example 1

Table 5.1 is an example from a simplified income statement (also known as a profit and loss statement or P&L).

Table 5.1. Simplified Income Statement

		As a % of gross revenue
Gross revenue	$687,000	100%
Cost of goods sold	$350,000	
Gross profit	$337,000	
Other variable costs	$25,000	
Contribution margin	$312,000	45.4%
Fixed costs	$292,000	
Pretax profit	$20,000	2.9%

Using the breakeven formula, BE = Fixed Costs ÷ Contribution Margin Ratio, we can calculate the breakeven point in dollars like this:

$$BE = FC \div CM\%$$

$$BE = \$292,000 \div 0.454$$

$$BE = \$642,962.$$

Interpreting the Result

In our hypothetical restaurant we must sell at least $642,962 (or round-ing it up to a nice round figure $643,000) during the relevant period to break even. Some restaurants earn far more than this. When the overall economy slumps, revenue in the full-service restaurant indus-try also declines as more people decide to eat at home. Changing eco-nomic conditions are all the more reason to monitor breakeven point and make adjustments as needed. Restaurants that are in the middle of the industry in terms of average check per customer are getting profits squeezed as competitive rivalry increases in the market segments below and above them. Another economic dimension that adds to the ratio-nale for monitoring breakeven in this particular industry is that even in a strong economy the overall growth rate of demand is low. Competi-tion for the restaurant dollar can be intense in some markets.

Fixed costs for a restaurant include marketing expenses, manager's salary and benefits, general administrative expenses, telephone, Internet, cable TV, interest, licenses, bank charges, utilities, repairs, insurance, occupancy costs such as rent, maintenance, janitorial services, depreciation, and other operating expenses. In some restaurants music and entertainment might be considered fixed costs. In other restaurants these might be variable costs.

For most restaurants variable costs include not only the cost of food and beverage products (COGS), since these vary directly with the volume of customers served, but also the cost of direct labor and benefits represented by servers, server helpers, cooks, hosts, temporary workers, and shift managers. Franchise royalties are also a variable cost since these normally are tied to the volume of sales. Table coverings and place settings may be variable costs. If paper goods are used, these are disposable and therefore constitute a variable cost. If linen is used, laundry expenses are incurred. The number of employees also represents a limited capacity for sales. Delivery drivers and fuel costs also can be a variable expense. Employee time cards and the payroll system can be coded to reflect the variable cost nature of direct labor and benefits. This is important since it allows the manager to distinguish between fixed costs and variable costs.

Contribution margin in dollars is calculated as the difference between gross revenue and total variable costs. Contribution margin can then be estimated as a percentage of gross revenue. To calculate the CM percentage we start with gross revenue, subtract the cost of goods sold, and subtract the other variable costs. We then divide the remainder by the gross revenue.

To get this information readily, an important consideration for any business—including a restaurant—is the structure of the chart of accounts for the general ledger. Most accounting systems are structured to meet obligations to the Internal Revenue Service (IRS), which is good except that the IRS obligations do not, by themselves, consider the information needed to monitor a firm's breakeven point. Generally accepted accounting principles (GAAP) encourage accountants to structure the accounting information system so that auditing is transparent and straightforward. Sometimes the accounting system fails to take into consideration whether the structure of the accounting information supports breakeven analysis or not. If fixed costs and variable costs are difficult to identify, calculating the breakeven point is more difficult.

Here's an example of a small portion of a chart of accounts used to monitor revenue derived from the sale of food:

- Sales of food—retail

Rolled into this one line item may be a lot of detail. For example, notice the difference between this item and the following list that divides the revenue by meal period and category of food:

- Entree sales breakfast
- Entree sales breakfast takeout
- Beverage sales breakfast
- Beverage sales breakfast takeout
- Dessert sales breakfast
- Dessert sales breakfast takeout
- Entree sales lunch
- Entree sales lunch takeout
- Beverage sales lunch (nonalcoholic)
- Beverage sales lunch takeout (nonalcoholic)
- Salad sales lunch
- Salad sales lunch takeout
- Dessert sales lunch
- Dessert sales lunch takeout
- Entree sales dinner
- Entree sales dinner takeout
- Beverage sales dinner
- Beverage sales dinner takeout
- Salad sales dinner
- Salad sales dinner takeout
- Dessert sales dinner
- Dessert sales dinner takeout
- Liquor sales lunch
- Beer sales lunch
- Wine sales lunch
- Liquor sales dinner
- Beer sales dinner
- Wine sales dinner

A level of detail can be added for classifying sales by location (dining room, coffee shop, grill, patio, drive-through, banquets) if this is relevant to what the restaurant offers. With the chart of accounts structured this way, information can be aggregated by mealtime or by product category. Most computerized cash register systems available these days can handle this level of detail. Of course, depending on the type of restaurant there might be other revenue streams such as souvenirs or sale of food at catered events. The point here is that the business owner can make an informed judgment about the level of detail to capture for analysis.

Cost of goods sold can also be expanded to include the various categories of food products and labor expenses. For example, the following might be used in one segment of the chart of accounts:

- Food costs—entrees
- Food costs—beverages
- Food costs—salads
- Food costs—desserts
- Carryout supplies
- Linen
- Paper/disposables

Direct labor can be classified according to the meal period worked.

Having good information is vital. For example, a restaurant owner may choose to provide an incentive for servers to promote a particular type of menu item that offers a good contribution margin. Traditionally, desserts are high-profit items in full-service restaurants. Incentives can change the product mix of an organization, shifting the breakeven point up or down. But without adequate information about the breakeven point, the incentive system may inadvertently incentivize employee behavior that undermines profitability.

Benefits

Several benefits to the COGS approach can be noted.[2] One of the benefits of this approach is that the data comes right from the income statement. An income statement can be produced on a monthly basis. It is a report that is readily available. No new data needs to be developed to use this method, and the information is aggregated over a relevant time period. This approach gives the restaurant owner an overall target of gross revenue to shoot for.

Sales dollars is the most common element of measure in any business. Sooner or later all productive work and production measures will be converted to sales dollars. Sales binds together the breakeven point and the income statement.

If we know (or expect) a certain proportion of our gross revenue will be generated by serving breakfast, another proportion by serving lunch, and another proportion by serving dinner, we can set some sales targets for the restaurant for these three mealtimes. For example, we might determine that in our market we generate 20% of our revenue at breakfast ($128,600), 30% at lunch ($192,900), and 50% at dinner ($321,500). We can set sales targets and design marketing promotional campaigns accordingly. Like all restaurants do, we will work vigorously to fine-tune the labor portion of the fixed costs for the three mealtimes.

We can break down the breakeven revenue on a per-day and per-meal-period basis. At this point we might want to employ our knowledge of the average per-plate revenue at breakfast, at lunch, and at dinner. Such information can then be used to estimate the number of customers we must serve at breakfast, lunch, and dinner to break even and the number of support staff needed to accomplish this. Informing employees of this can help them understand the reason behind the need to serve customers in a timely manner, clean up, and prepare for serving more customers at each mealtime.

For example, if we estimate that the average per-plate revenue at breakfast is $7.25, we will need to serve 1,187 breakfast customers during the relevant period of time. If the average per-plate revenue at lunch is $9.50, we will need to serve 2,030 lunch customers. If the average per-plate revenue at dinner is $15.75, we will need to serve 2,041 customers at dinner. Naturally, we will review the amount of seating space in the restaurant to make sure that our capacity can adequately serve this number of people.

Another way a restaurant can analyze the operational impact on breakeven is by the traditional categories of beverages, salads, entrees, and desserts, meaning by product category rather than by the type of meal served. With close analysis the contribution margin of each product category can be estimated. The operational ability to prepare and serve each category of food is at the core of the business.

Breakeven thinking can be extended into the operations in this type of business by considering the mix of tables or service areas provided. For example, if your restaurant only has booths seating six people each, and you have 20 booths, you could be limiting your ability to break even since a single customer coming in will tie up a whole booth. Having a mix of tables allows for groups of different sizes to eat at the restaurant.[3]

Limitations

Like all methods of estimating breakeven, this approach has its limitations. The cost of goods sold method, like other methods, depends on having accurate historical information. It is *retrospective* in its perspective. Using this approach to look to the future to estimate the breakeven point depends heavily on your assumptions. If you are using assumptions based on recent past history, you must assume future consumer behavior will continue relatively unchanged into the immediate future (into the next relevant, short-term period of time for which breakeven needs to be estimated). This method calculates breakeven in terms of dollars of gross revenue but not the number of units sold. We can estimate the number of units sold (customers served) to break even, but such an estimate will have a margin of error that is unacceptable in a highly price-competitive market where customers are more price sensitive.

For every business that sells more than one product or service, the issue of sales mix or product mix affects the breakeven point. The broad COGS approach does not attempt to take into account the sales mix. For some businesses, the fluctuation in sales mix from day to day or week to week can be great. This variation has a direct impact on the variability of the breakeven point. The greater the variability of the breakeven point, the greater the risk that managers will not have the information needed to make timely decisions as conditions change.

By itself, the cost of goods sold approach does not tell you how the breakeven point changes with volume of sales or as the scale of capacity changes. This reflects a related weakness of the COGS approach: it can be seen as superficial and lacks a level of detail to provide alert management with good information to control profitability.

Although sales dollars is the most common element tracked by a business, the sales dollar cannot be applied with ease to all departments. For example, maintenance and janitorial services are only indirectly linked with sales dollars. This doesn't mean that the cleanliness and operational effectiveness of a restaurant are unimportant for generating sales. Indeed, cleanliness is one of the reasons customers will come back to a restaurant.

CHAPTER 6

Modified Breakeven Analysis
Factoring Estimates of Demand

We know selling price plays an important part in determining the breakeven point. With everything else unchanged, the lower the price, the higher the breakeven point and vice versa. Cost is an important factor that influences price. In fact, we can say that price is never completely separated from cost considerations. With everything else unchanged, the higher the costs the more managers will be inclined to raise the price and vice versa. Price in its relationship to cost is important, but it is not the only factor to consider.

For most products and services offered in competitive markets, managers must take into consideration the competition and how customer behaviors might change if the price changes. For some products a small percent increase in price can make a significant difference in whether the company is able to break even. But what impact will increasing the price have on customers' willingness to buy when substitute products are readily available? In other words, how will demand change if the price changes?

The traditional breakeven formula is a cost-based approach. It is silent regarding the influence of demand on breakeven. In this chapter we will review a modified breakeven analysis method that factors in estimates of demand.[1] To do this we will first review the basic idea of demand. We will then review some approaches to estimating demand and customer responsiveness to price changes. Finally, we will see how to use estimates of demand to calculate the breakeven point and in the process find the "sweet spot" of optimal profit.

Demand

Demand is an estimate of the volume of a product or service that customers are willing to buy at different levels of price.[2] For most products and services, if the price falls, we expect that customers are more willing and able to purchase a higher quantity than they would otherwise purchase.

Visually we represent this price-demand relationship (Figure 6.1) with a downward-sloping line on a graph where price is on the vertical axis and quantity demanded is on the horizontal axis.

Demand is driven by several factors: consumer tastes, the number of buyers in the market, income, prices of substitutes and complementary goods, and customer expectations. For example, in the early 1980s when people began to see the power of personal computers (PCs), consumer tastes began to shift away from the use of typewriters. This occurred even though at the time the electric typewriters used in most businesses were becoming sophisticated enough to help the typist correct errors. Printers had not yet developed to the point where letter-quality printing could be created on the same page as graphics. Over a period of just a few years, demand for electric typewriters began to shift and all but die out as demand for PCs dramatically increased. This became a shift in the demand curves of both typewriters and personal computers. Using Figure 6.1, the demand curve for typewriters began to shift to the left as the demand curve for personal computers began to shift to the right.

As managers saw the power of personal computers and software applications were developed to increase efficiency, most companies were willing and able to purchase at least one personal computer. But as workers began to envision how the personal computer could make their work more efficient, interest began to grow and company managers were more willing to spend money on this product. As the price of PCs began to

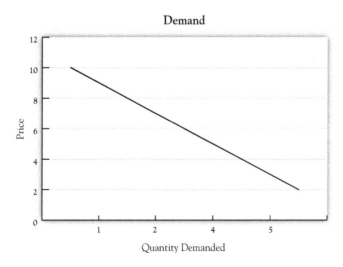

Figure 6.1. Price-Demand Relationship

drop, companies were willing and able to buy more PCs. This became movement along the demand curve.

The question managers had to deal with was this: If the price changed, how responsive would customers be in terms of their willingness and ability to purchase a personal computer? As with most products and services, the presence of readily available substitute products is the primary influence on customer responsiveness to price changes.[3] We sometimes talk about responsiveness to price changes in terms of *price elasticity of demand.* If there are few readily available substitutes and customers want the product, producers can increase the price and customers will continue in their willingness to purchase. In contrast, if there are many readily available substitute products and customers want the product, producers who increase the price will find that customers will switch to a substitute. Another way of seeing this is to say that if companies are unable or unwilling to make their product different from substitute products along the lines that customers find important, then price becomes more important to customers and they are more willing to stop buying the higher priced product in favor of the lower priced product.

Recall that the breakeven point is the point at which total revenue equals total costs. The impact of customer responsiveness on total revenue is important. When prices increase and customers are responsive to price changes because of readily available substitutes, some customers switch to a lower price competitor product and total revenue decreases, making the breakeven point more difficult to achieve. When prices decrease relative to competitors' prices and customers are responsive to price changes, some customers begin to switch away from competitors. This increases total revenue, making the breakeven point easier to achieve.

When customers are less responsive to price changes, increasing the price can result in an increase in total revenue, making the breakeven point easier to achieve. Under these conditions, lowering the price will result in lowering total revenue.

Estimating Demand and Customer Responsiveness

The challenge these principles present to the manager is how to estimate demand and customer responsiveness to changes in price. It is not always easy to obtain an accurate estimate of demand.[4] Table 6.1 provides a summary of some of the approaches.

Table 6.1. Methods for Estimating Demand

Method	Advantages	Disadvantages
Intuition: Study the microeconomic structure of the market, and estimate the responsiveness based on the number and availability of close substitutes. The more substitutes, the more responsiveness.	Informed by years of experience in the relevant market, intuition can be a powerful decision-making tool. Rooted in economic theory. Externally focused.	Decision makers tend to be overly optimistic when estimating customer behaviors. Customers are viewed as acting favorably toward the company. The less market experience a person has, the more likely intuition will be inaccurate.
Simple History: Compare demand for the product this year at this year's prices with demand for each of the previous three years at previous years' prices.	Historical data is readily available.	One time period may have little connection with a current or future time period since economic conditions and market structures change. Demand is likely to be overestimated or underestimated.
Secondary Research: Find published results of empirical research regarding customer responsiveness for a particular product category.	Provides a general awareness for an industry as a whole. When information is available, it saves the company a lot of time and the expense of primary research.	Secondary research may not answer the question about the responsiveness that a particular company faces. Customer responsiveness across an industry is very different from responsiveness to a particular company's pricing policies. The market conditions present when the research was completed may be out of date.
Primary Research: Survey or interview customers to determine the likelihood of purchasing actions changing if price changes. This method can also provide a general estimate of the relative importance of price—information that can inform intuition.	A focused set of questions allows the company to get detailed information about a specific product and pricing levels that are of concern.	There can be a gap between what the customer says he or she would do and what they actually do.

(*continued on next page*)

Table 6.1. Methods for Estimating Demand (continued)

Method	Advantages	Disadvantages
Market Experiment: Select a product and a portion of the market. Increase or decrease the price, and see what happens to customer demand.	Data from actual consumer behaviors are observed under real conditions where price is changed. Real marketplace data (rather than "guestimates") are highly valuable. Statistical tests can be used to determine whether the results are by chance or because of the experiment.	Pricing experiments for a small company or a one-product company carry the risk that the total revenue will fall below an acceptable level if customers are more responsive than expected. A market experiment is usually done on a small scale, weakening the general applicability of results to the whole market. A market experiment can cause competitors to act in a way that is unfavorable. Raising price gives competitors the opportunity to exploit the price difference. Lowering price can touch off a price war. In either case, you could lose customers!
Regression Analysis: Regression analysis should take into account the price of the product, the disposable income of consumers, the price that competitors are charging, and the amount of money spent on marketing promotion.[5]	This is considered to be one of the best methods since it is based on powerful statistical tests.	Busy managers who do not work with statistics on a daily basis may find interpreting test results too daunting a task. Getting accurate historical data may be difficult.

None of the methods of estimating demand is perfect. But for some of the methods there are workarounds. For example, in a market experiment one way around the disadvantage is to test different price packages simultaneously, monitoring the differences in demand that result. For example, a company might have three different offers in the market: (a) a two-for-one deal, (b) a straight percent discount, and (c) a coupon giving access to a different price.[6] When conducting primary research, managers can ask customers how likely it is that the customer will buy less of a product sold by the company if the price changes by a specific percent point.

Factoring Demand in Breakeven Analysis

The result you want to achieve from market analysis described previously is an estimate of demand at different levels of price. For example, take a company whose fixed costs are $260,000 for the period and unit variable cost is $3.25. After market analysis, managers determine that at different prices (ranging from a low of $21 to a high of $29) demand changes from a low of 9,000 units at the higher price to a high of 14,500 units at the lower price. The "demand schedule" in Figure 6.2 illustrates the model offered by Kurtz.[7]

The data from this table can be graphed as shown in Figure 6.3, Optimal Profit Graph. You will notice from the table and graph that the firm can be profitable when charging anywhere between $22 and $27 per unit. Knowing this, managers will naturally wonder where the best price is to achieve the most demand and the highest profit. In this case, everything else remaining equal, optimal profit is attained when the unit price is $24.

Notice that as the price declines, the breakeven point increases, as we would expect. Notice also that this particular company can lose money if it charges a price so high that demand drops too low. It also can lose

	A	B	C	D	E	F	G	H
1	EXAMPLE DEMAND SCHEDULE							
2								
3		Quantity					Breakeven	Total
4		Demanded	Total	Total	Total	Total	Point	Profit or
5	Price	In Units	Revenue	Fixed Cost	Var Costs	Costs	In Units	(Loss)
6	$29	9,000	$261,000	$260,000	$29,250	$289,250	10,097	($28,250)
7	27	11,000	297,000	260,000	35,750	295,750	10,947	1,250
8	26	11,600	301,600	260,000	37,700	297,700	11,429	3,900
9	25	12,250	306,250	260,000	39,813	299,813	11,954	6,438
10	24	13,000	312,000	260,000	42,250	302,250	12,530	9,750
11	23	13,500	310,500	260,000	43,875	303,875	13,165	6,625
12	22	14,000	308,000	260,000	45,500	305,500	13,867	2,500
13	21	14,500	304,500	260,000	47,125	307,125	14,648	(2,625)
14								
15	Within the profitable price range (between $27 to $22) demand changes by:							27%

Figure 6.2. Demand Schedule

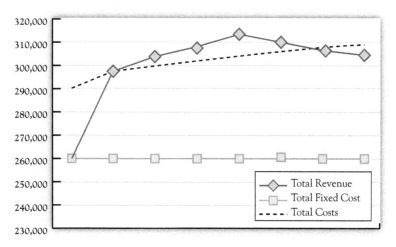

Figure 6.3. Optimal Profit Graph

money if it charges $21—a price too low, even though the quantity demanded goes up. To a manager, the difference between prices of $21 and $22 may not seem significant. Likewise, the difference between $27 and $29 doesn't seem to be great. It is just under 7.5%. The problem is that this particular price jump puts the firm in the position that it has just priced itself out of a profitable market. If the market analysis is accurate, even small differences in price can have a big impact on consumers.

Managers will have to ask themselves important questions. Does capacity exist to support the achievement of optimum profit? If the current price is $26 and we choose to maximize profit by lowering it to just $24, what will be the competitor responses, and how will price changes of competitors affect demand for our product at the $24 price? If our price is $22 and we raise it to $24, will competitors attempt to take advantage of this through marketing promotion? If so, will this adversely affect demand for our product?

An Alternative

As Smith and Nagle[8] point out, precise estimates of actual price responsiveness are extremely difficult to obtain for many businesses. Smith and Nagle propose beginning with managers making hypothetical proposed price changes, calculating the breakeven point for each, and then estimating the degree of responsiveness (price elasticity of demand) customers are likely to have to such price proposals.

The first step is to calculate the breakeven point for a product (using the traditional breakeven analysis formula) at different levels of price. For example, Table 6.2, Breakeven Points at Different Price Levels, might be constructed for a corporation.

The selling price (SP) of $80 was chosen in this illustration. Using information from the table, a graph can be drawn showing the breakeven points at different levels of price. Construct the graph, plotting the price on the vertical axis and the unit sales volume on the horizontal axis. The line drawn through each of the breakeven points on the graph becomes the "constant profit" curve, or the line on which breakeven is achieved at each price level. See Figure 6.4, Constant Profit Curve at Various Prices.

In Figure 6.4, the price of $80 is the current price. At this price the breakeven sales volume is 50,000 units. To the constant profit curve can be added hypothetical demand curves illustrating the degree of responsiveness to price. One demand curve (labeled "A" in Figure 6.5, Inelastic Demand Curve) shows that customers are less responsive to price changes (relatively inelastic demand). To the right of the demand curve, losses will occur if prices are changed in this direction (reduced). To the left of the demand curve, gains will occur if prices are changed in this direction (increased).

Table 6.2. Breakeven Points at Different Price Levels

% Δ in SP	SP ($)	CM2 ($)	BE_U	% Change BE Sales	Change in Units
25.0%	100	40	25,000	−50.0%	−25,000
20.0%	96	36	27,778	−44.4%	−22,222
15.0%	92	32	31,250	−37.5%	−18,750
10.0%	88	28	35,714	−28.6%	−14,286
5.0%	84	24	41,667	−16.7%	−8,333
0.0%	80	20	50,000	0.0%	0
−5.0%	76	16	62,500	25.0%	12,500
−10.0%	72	12	83,333	66.7%	33,333
−15.0%	68	8	125,000	150.0%	5,000
−20.0%	64	4	250,000	400.0%	200,000

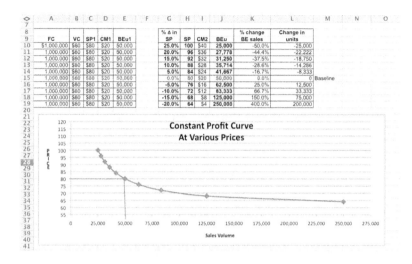

	A	B	C	D	E	F	G	H	I	J	K	L	M	N	O
7															
8							% Δ in				% change	Change in			
9	FC	VC	SP1	CM1	BEu1		SP	SP	CM2	BEu	BE sales	units			
10	$1,000,000	$60	$80	$20	50,000		25.0%	100	$40	25,000	-50.0%	-25,000			
11	1,000,000	$60	$80	$20	50,000		20.0%	96	$36	27,778	-44.4%	-22,222			
12	1,000,000	$60	$80	$20	50,000		15.0%	92	$32	31,250	-37.5%	-18,750			
13	1,000,000	$60	$80	$20	50,000		10.0%	88	$28	35,714	-28.6%	-14,286			
14	1,000,000	$60	$80	$20	50,000		5.0%	84	$24	41,667	-16.7%	-8,333			
15	1,000,000	$60	$80	$20	50,000		0.0%	80	$20	50,000	0.0%	0	Baseline		
16	1,000,000	$60	$80	$20	50,000		-5.0%	76	$16	62,500	25.0%	12,500			
17	1,000,000	$60	$80	$20	50,000		-10.0%	72	$12	83,333	66.7%	33,333			
18	1,000,000	$60	$80	$20	50,000		-15.0%	68	$8	125,000	150.0%	75,000			
19	1,000,000	$60	$80	$20	50,000		-20.0%	64	$4	250,000	400.0%	200,000			

Figure 6.4. Constant Profit Curve at Various Prices

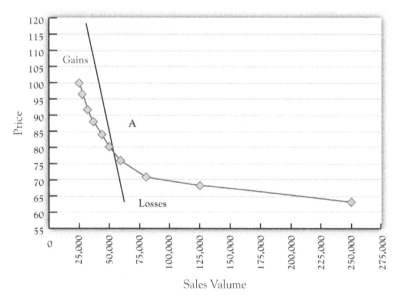

Figure 6.5. Inelastic Demand Curve

Notice that the demand curve "A" crosses the constant profit curve when price equals $80 (the current price). If the price is changed, the current price becomes the "baseline" against which customer responsiveness must be evaluated.

The other hypothetical demand curve shown below indicates more responsiveness to price changes. The demand curve "B" in Figure 6.6, Elastic Demand Curve, is flatter than demand curve "A" in Figure 6.5. The flatter demand curve illustrates that when prices are increased above $80, losses will likely occur since customers are more responsive to price increases. But when prices are reduced below $80, more customers will buy the product, and as a result gains will be achieved.

The benefit of using this type of graph over attempting to calculate the precise demand is that the manager simply has to make an informed judgment as to whether customer responsiveness is likely to be greater or less than the level required to achieve breakeven.

Table 6.2 and Figures 6.4 through 6.6 put forward by Smith and Nagle still require managers to make an informed judgment regarding the price elasticity of demand (customer responsiveness to changes in price)—the slope of the demand curve. The marginal advantage their approach provides during managerial discussions is that the table and graphs will encourage dialog and debate over the assumptions regarding customer responsiveness at various hypothetical prices.

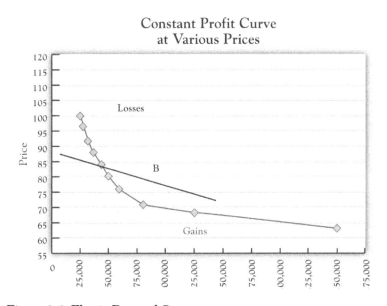

Figure 6.6. Elastic Demand Curve

The Ethical Dimension

If customers continue to buy a product even though the price goes up, everything else being equal, total revenue and total profit will increase. Such an action may provide a short-run economic payoff. In the long run, any of several things will probably happen. First, some customers will find out about this and turn against the company, creating demand for a substitute. Second, even though the availability of substitutes is low, other customers will just not purchase, choosing to go without and wait for a substitute. Third, this action will entice competitors into the market. In any case, if customers choose to sit out or if more competitors enter the market, market prices and industry profits will tend to go down. Thus company managers who try to capture too much short-run profit may very likely find that they have unintentionally brought about the demise of the very thing they hoped to achieve.

Considering customer responsiveness has an important ethical dimension. For example, if company managers determine that customers are relatively unresponsive to changes in price because few readily available substitutes are present in the market, is it moral for those managers to take advantage of the situation in order to capture more revenue by raising the price even if their costs remain unchanged? It can be argued that to use the degree of customer responsiveness against customers by raising prices above what would be reasonably expected is unethical.

We have already introduced the idea that many companies sell more than just one product. We turn next to consider another approach to handling this type of situation.

CHAPTER 7

Dealing With Changes in Product Mix Using Weighted Averages

As we have seen, product mix is one of the most important influences on breakeven point. Change the product mix, and if there are wide differences in variable costs and selling prices in the mix, the profitability can change quickly.

In this chapter we will focus on two breakeven methods that employ weighted averages. The first is the weighted average contribution margin method, and the second is the weighted average selling prices method.

The Formula

The product mix can be used to determine the weighted average contribution margin as is shown in the following formula:

$$\text{Breakeven Units (BE}_U) = \text{Fixed Costs} \div \text{Weighted Average Contribution Margin.}$$

Breakeven and cost-volume-profit analysis are typically explained and illustrated with single-product or single-service organizations. In reality, most organizations offer more than one product or service. We refer to these multiple products or services as the sales mix. We need a method to apply cost-volume-profit analysis to commercial reality.

An appliance store, for example, might track sales of various brands and types of appliance (refrigerators, ranges, dishwashers, etc.). It might also track repair service on appliance brands, warranty and out-of-warranty service, and service on different types of appliances. Each of these sources of revenue could produce a different contribution margin (CM). Let's look at an example.

Example 1

Bob's Appliances has provided us with the data in Table 7.1, Sales Mix.

After calculating the weighted average contribution margin, the breakeven calculation is the same:

$$\frac{\$448,400 \text{ Bob's Annual Fixed Costs}}{\$236 \text{ Weighted Average CM}} = \begin{array}{l} 1,900 \text{ Total Units to} \\ \text{Be Sold Annually.} \end{array}$$

However, the 1,900 units to be sold to break even must be sold in the proportions stated in the sales mix: 950 refrigerators (1,900 × 50%), 380 dishwashers (1,900 × 20%), and 570 repair service calls (1,900 × 30%).[1]

Using Table 7.2, Sales Mix Quantities to Be Sold, we can check to be sure these sales quantities will bring Bob to break even. If Bob adds a desired profit, the calculation is

$$\frac{\$448,400 \text{ Annual Fixed Costs} + \$17,700 \text{ Desired Profit}}{\$236 \text{ Weighted Average CM}} = \begin{array}{l} 1,975 \text{ Units to Be} \\ \text{Sold Annually.} \end{array}$$

One of our limiting assumptions of cost-volume-profit analysis is that the sales mix must remain constant for the results to be meaningful. Let's examine what happens to Bob's Appliances if his sales mix changes (Table 7.3, Changing Sales Mix). Bob sold the overall total units required, 1,900, but because he sold more low contribution margin units and fewer high contribution margin units (the sales mix changed), he failed to achieve breakeven.

Table 7.1. Sales Mix

	Sales mix	CM per unit	Weighted CM
Refrigerators	50%	$350	$175 = ($350 × 50%)
Dishwashers	20%	$200	$40 = ($200 × 20%)
Repair service calls	30%	$70	$21 = ($70 × 30%)
Weighted average CM			$236

Table 7.2. Sales Mix Quantities to Be Sold

	Units sold	CM per unit	Total CM earned
Refrigerators	950	$350	$332,500 ($350 × 950)
Dishwashers	380	$200	$76,000 ($200 × 380)
Repair service calls	570	$70	$39,900 ($70 × 570)
Total units sold	1,900		
Total CM earned			$448,400
Fixed costs			$448,400
Net income or loss			$0

Table 7.3. Changing Sales Mix

	Units sold	CM per unit	Total CM earned
Refrigerators	850	$350	$297,500 ($350 × 850)
Dishwashers	480	$200	$96,000 ($200 × 480)
Repair service calls	570	$70	$39,900 ($70 × 570)
Total units sold	1,900 (as indicated by the breakeven calculation)		
Total CM earned			$433,400
Fixed costs			$448,400
Net loss			($15,000)

Benefits

For some companies circumstances may make it difficult for managers to identify unit variable costs. A company that sells dozens or even scores of different products might employ a spreadsheet or other computer software to make the calculations less tedious. Once the spreadsheet is set up, sensitivity analysis can be used to monitor the impact on breakeven if demand changes for certain products or packages of products.

As with other methods, thinking about breakeven naturally should lead directly to thinking about operations. The more products a company produces, the more managers will be interested in finding synergies between these products so that production is achieved by sharing critical resources across more than one product. Such synergies have the potential of lowering costs, making the breakeven point easier to achieve.

In some situations or companies, managers choose not to go through the time and expense of identifying unit variable costs. These managers might benefit from the next method highlighted in this chapter: weighted average selling price.

Weighted Average Selling Price Method

For organizations that sell essentially one service but at different prices, breakeven can be calculated even if the unit variable costs are not known. Because of the differences in prices, the product mix still heavily influences the breakeven point. For example, a minor league baseball club sells essentially the same entertainment "product" to all who attend its home games but at three different prices for children, adults, and senior citizens. Differential pricing is usually charged for seat location in the ballpark. The Grand Ole Opry sells tickets to the same event but at different prices depending on location of seating. A hotel rents rooms but at different prices depending on the season of the year or the distribution channels used in marketing. Airlines sell seats on flights at different prices depending on season, timing of purchase, and the marketing organization used to sell tickets. Such managers may choose this approach to focus on the marketing side of the business.

Like total sales revenue, the unit selling price is often known when other details are not as readily known. Total costs may be known when variable costs cannot be distinguished from fixed costs. Under these conditions the weighted average selling price method can be useful.

The Formula

The weighted average selling price method allows for the calculation of breakeven using the following formula:

$$BE_U = \text{Total Costs} \div \text{Weighted Average Selling Price.}$$

Notice in this method that we are comparing company total costs as a whole group and selling price of the company's products as a weighted group. Total costs, for most companies, requires a straightforward process of simply summing all costs for a relevant period of time. Unlike other breakeven formulas, no distinction is made between fixed costs and variable costs.

Weighting the selling price is accomplished by taking each product and multiplying its selling price by the proportion of the total units sold. This is the weighted selling price for one product. The sum of the weighted selling prices for all products is the weighted average selling price for the company's products as a group.

Note that calculating a weighted average is not the same as calculating the simple average. For example, see Table 7.4, Comparison of Simple and Weighted Average Selling Price, listing four products and the selling price (SP) for each.

Simple average (also known as the mean) selling price (SP) is calculated by adding the four selling prices and dividing by the number of different products (in this case, there are four) offered in the market. In Table 7.4 the simple average is $59.95. *Weighted* average selling price is $4 less than the simple average selling price. In this case, using the simple average price would *underestimate* the breakeven point. In another case, the weighted average selling price might be more than the simple average, in which case the breakeven point would be *overestimated* if the simple average were used.

Now let's use this in a couple of examples.

Example 2

For 20 years Olympia Community Theater has been selling tickets to its annual 3-week production of *Fiddler on the Roof*. The Board of Trustees for Olympia has decided that this year Olympia should sell tickets at three different prices: $6 (children), $10 (adults), and $8 (senior citizens). For the production, Olympia Community Theater Company rents the old and quite small (125 seats) Paramount Theater. It also rents

Table 7.4. Comparison of Simple and Weighted Average Selling Price

Products	SP	Sales mix	Weighted Average SP
Royal	$29.95	35.0%	$10.48
Excelsior	$49.95	25.0%	$12.49
Galaxy	$69.95	15.0%	$10.49
Ultra	$89.95	25.0%	$22.49
TOTAL		100.0%	$55.95
Simple average	$59.95		

props, lighting equipment, and costumes, using these resources for a total of 15 performances of the play. Several thousand dollars are spent on promotional materials including the printing of the program, tickets, and posters. Olympia also pays an honorarium to local musicians who participate in the pit orchestra. Total costs for the production equal $12,650. The question the producer wants answered is, how many tickets must we sell to break even?

The weighted average selling price is shown in Table 7.5, Weighted Average Ticket Price. Sales mix is based on historical trends over the last two decades.

With this information, the breakeven point is calculated as follows:

$$CT = \text{Total Costs}$$

$$SPWT = \text{Weighted Average Selling Price}$$

$$BE_U = CT \div SPWT = \text{Number of Tickets Sold to Break Even}$$

$$BE_U = \$12,650 \div \$8.80$$

$$BE_U = 1,438 \text{ Tickets Sold.}$$

Over a 3-week period with five shows produced each week, the average attendance needs to be represented by 96 tickets sold for each show. This is 77% of capacity. Using the historical trend data on sales mix, we can see that to break even on its production of *Fiddler on the Roof,* Olympia will sell 288 tickets for children, 863 adult tickets, and 288 tickets to senior citizens.

Example 3

Consider Peninsula Consulting, a professional financial service organization that offers four levels of service to privately owned businesses each at a different price: $2,295 (Basic), $2,995 (Advanced), $3,495 (Silver), and

Table 7.5. Weighted Average Ticket Price

	Children	Adults	Seniors	Total
Sales mix	20%	60%	20%	100%
SP	$6	$10	$8	
Wtd. average SP	$1.20	$6	$1.60	$8.80

$3,995 (Platinum). Small businesses "subscribe" annually to receive advice on finance issues throughout the year, assistance with year-end taxes, and production of year-end financial statements. To deliver the promised services, Peninsula Consulting incurs total costs of $950,000 annually. The sales mix is shown in Table 7.6, Peninsula Consulting Sales Mix.

The weighted average selling price is $2,965 per service package. To break even, Peninsula Consulting must sell a total of 320 service packages at the given sales mix.

Interpreting the Result

Similar to the contribution margin method considered elsewhere in this book, the weighted average selling price method casts the result in terms of units of product or service sold. Because of this, breakeven analysis should lead managers naturally to think about the operational issues such as capacity, staffing, marketing, and organization. In the previous example, if Peninsula Consulting learns that it is easier to sell Basic Service packages and very difficult to sell Platinum Service packages, the sales mix and the breakeven point will most likely change.

As the top managers of Peninsula staff and organize the company, they must ask what staffing mix is required to provide Basic Service to 120 clients, Advanced Service to 80 clients, Silver Service to 64 clients, and Platinum Service to 48 clients. For example, the number of accounting professionals and their support staff needed to provide Platinum Service for every 10 clients may be quite different from that required to provide Basic Service.

Anytime sales mix (also known as product mix) is factored into breakeven analysis, the need for accurate and timely data becomes vital. Managers who use this method must closely track sales mix. As actual

Table 7.6. Peninsula Consulting Sales Mix

	Basic Service	Advanced Service	Silver Service	Platinum Service	Total
Sales mix	40%	25%	20%	15%	100%
SP	$2,295	$2,995	$3,495	$3,995	
Wtd. Average SP	$918	$749	$699	$599	$2,965

sales mix deviates from the expected, managers must make adjustments in operations, marketing, or both. Some managerial adjustments may involve increasing commitment to fixed costs, which, in turn, have an impact on breakeven.

This method may be especially useful at the beginning of a venture, when total costs can be estimated and market pricing is known.

Benefits

This method places weighted average selling price in the spotlight. Because of this, it speaks the language of marketing and sales. The simplicity of rolling all costs together into one round total-cost number is attractive. This eliminates the need for detailed cost-accounting work to identify unit variable costs. With this method there is no need to differentiate between fixed costs and variable costs.

The weighted average selling price method can be used in a setting where broad-scope numbers are being discussed, such as the total cost of a start-up organization. Relatively quick calculations can be made "on the back of an envelope" and used in discussion of assumptions and strategy.

Limitations

Since variable costs are not factored into this method, it is silent with respect to variable costs. Therefore, calculating the result does not naturally lead a manager to think about the cost structure and what can be done to improve that structure. Eliminating the topic of variable costs from the discussion can unintentionally lead managers away from analyzing opportunities for improving the cost structure.

Another limitation is that this method, while relatively simple to use for a company offering a few different products, is cumbersome for companies that sell many different kinds of products. Capturing unit sales information is imperative for calculating an accurate sales mix. A spreadsheet or relational database should be used in these situations since it can reduce the cumbersome nature of the calculations in cases where many products are offered.

When this method is used to help project the expected future experience of an organization, the whole exercise will turn on the accuracy of the assumptions regarding total costs and the assumptions about market prices and sales mix. Inaccuracies in these assumptions will drive spurious breakeven analysis results.

CHAPTER 8

High-Low Method

For costs that are neither purely variable nor purely fixed, we must identify and separate those variable and fixed components to be able to incorporate them into our cost-volume-profit analysis. The high-low method is a simple way to accomplish that objective.

We will continue with the example of Bob's Appliances. Bob delivers the new appliances he sells to customers. Some of the costs associated with this delivery service are fixed, such as insurance, emissions inspections for his trucks, and depreciation. Other costs, such as gasoline and tires, are variable, based on the number of deliveries he makes and the miles he travels per year. In the most current year, Bob made 180 deliveries and incurred a total delivery cost of $2,800. These will be our "high" values. In the immediately preceding year, Bob made 140 deliveries and incurred an annual delivery cost of $2,500. These will be our "low" values. Begin the analysis by expressing the data this way:[1]

$2,800 Current Year Costs – $2,500 Preceding Year Costs = $300
Change in Costs

180 Current Year Deliveries – 140 Preceding Year Deliveries = 40
Change in Deliveries

Variable Cost per Delivery = $300 ÷ 40 = $7.50

To find the fixed cost component, use the "high" values: 180 deliveries and $2,800 costs.

Total Costs = $2,800

Total Variable Costs = (180 Deliveries × $7.50 Variable Cost
per Delivery) = $1,350

Total Fixed Costs per Year = $2,800 – $1,350 = $1,450

Some people find that organizing the data into a matrix is useful in making the calculation as illustrated in Table 8.1, High-Low Example. Use the same method as shown previously to find the fixed cost amount.

You may be presented with daily, weekly, monthly, or other periodic data. You may have a large amount of data to work with. However, the high-low method always uses only the highest unit or activity value and the lowest unit or activity value. All other data are disregarded. This feature of the high-low method makes it subject to misinformation if the high or low values are anomalies (statistically referred to as outliers). If the high cost value is unusually large or the low cost value is unusually small, the variable cost per unit will be overstated and the total fixed cost will be understated. Table 8.2, Outlier Example, is an illustration of the effect of an outlier.

The variable cost per unit, in the outlier example, is overstated by $5 per unit. What about the fixed cost per year?

Total Costs = $3,000 (Outlier Cost Amount)

Less Total Variable Costs = *$2,250* (180 Deliveries × $12.50 Variable Cost per Delivery)

Equals Total Fixed Costs = $750 per Year

Table 8.1. High-Low Example

	Cost	Units
High value	$2,800	180
Low value	$2,500	140
Difference	$300	40
Calculation	$300 ÷ 40 = $7.50 Variable Cost per Delivery	

Table 8.2. Outlier Example

	Cost	Units
High value*	$3,000	180
Low value	$2,500	140
Difference	$500	40
Calculation	*$500* ÷ 40 = $12.50 Variable Cost per Delivery	

*This cost amount is unusually high, an outlier.

Comparing the $1,450 annual fixed cost using normal values from our first example with the $750 annual fixed cost using an outlier value, the annual fixed cost, using the outlier value, is understated by almost half.

Another potential for misinterpretation is illustrated by Table 8.3, Maintenance Costs Versus Miles Driven.

The proper choice for the high value is the highest number of miles driven (the highest activity level). However, when placed in the formula, the data mathematically produce a negative value for variable cost per mile driven. The result is clearly unreasonable. You will need to choose a different time period for analysis or try grouping the months into quarters or years to avoid these nonsense results.

One of the limiting assumptions is that there is no inflation or deflation to distort the results. Inflation or deflation tends to cause fixed costs to appear to be variable costs. When evaluating costs that have fixed quantities associated with them (such as utilities or fuel consumed, lumber used, labor hours worked), the quantity of the item consumed may be used instead of the dollar cost to calculate the variable and fixed amounts. Then, a dollar amount is applied.

Statewide Industries uses large quantities of natural gas to produce its product. In the current year, it used 1,000,000 mcf (million cubic feet) to produce 800,000 units of finished product. In the immediately preceding year, the company used 920,000 mcf to produce 740,000 units of finished product. See Table 8.4 Natural Gas Use.

Table 8.3. Maintenance Costs Versus Miles Driven

	Maintenance cost	Miles driven
January	$1,000	11,200
February	$900	10,600
March	$800	11,300

Table 8.4. Natural Gas Use

	mcf	Units
High value	1,000,000	800,000
Low value	920,000	700,000
Difference	80,000	100,000
Calculation	80,000 ÷ 100,000 = 0.80 mcf Variable Usage (Cost) per Unit	

Table 8.5, Fixed Cost Calculation, illustrates the calculation of fixed usage.

After obtaining the variable and fixed rates, you may apply the appropriate cost per mcf. If the utility company is charging $2.40 per mcf, then your variable cost per unit would be (.8 mcf × $2.40) = $1.92. The fixed cost would be (360,000 mcf × $2.40) = $864,000.

One of the things we are trying to achieve with the high-low method is a separation of total (mixed) costs into a fixed cost component and a variable cost component. An alternative way of thinking about the relationship between the high and the low is this formula:

Total Mixed Costs = Fixed Cost Component + (Slope × Variable Cost Component).

Putting in the familiar algebra format, we get

$$Y = a + bX,$$

where

$$Y = \text{Total Mixed Costs}$$

$$a = \text{Fixed Cost Component}$$

$$b = \text{Unit Variable Cost Component (Slope of the Line)}$$

$$X = \text{Number of Units Produced and Sold.}$$

This formula depicts the relative differences in cost and volume as a linear relationship between the highest point and the lowest point in terms of values of cost and their corresponding activity levels. We can think of this method as employing the highest point of costs and the lowest point of costs with a sloped line that connects these two points.

Table 8.5. Fixed Cost Calculation

Total usage	1,000,000	mcf
Less total variable usage	640,000	(800,000 Units × 0.80 mcf variable usage per unit)
Equals total fixed usage	360,000	mcf

Example 1

Consider Table 8.6, Activity and Cost Data, from a company.

We will first calculate the unit variable cost as follows:

Unit Variable Costs (VC) = Change in Cost ÷ Change in Activity.

To calculate the change in cost, we will subtract the low-cost month from the high-cost month.

Change in Cost = $796,500 – $320,500 = $476,000

To calculate the change in activity, we subtract the low-cost month from the high-cost month.

Change in Activity = 629,600 Units – 159,500 Units = 470,100 Units

Now we divide the change in costs by the change in activity to estimate the unit variable cost (VC):

$$VC = 476,000 ÷ 470,100$$

$$VC = \$1.012.$$

Table 8.6. Activity and Cost Data

Month	Activity level	Mixed costs
January	255,000	$425,000
February	332,000	$536,000
March	159,500	$320,500
April	415,500	$643,200
May	375,500	$554,500
June	522,400	$689,800
July	629,600	$796,500
August	556,400	$710,500
September	439,700	$668,400
October	486,300	$685,200
November	351,400	$527,300
December	298,100	$447,800

The following are the high and low points from this period:

July	629,600	$796,500
March	159,500	$320,500

With this information we can estimate (separate) the fixed costs by using the information from July, the high production month.

$$\text{Total Costs} = \text{Fixed Costs} + \text{Variable Costs}$$

Therefore,

$$\text{Fixed Costs} = \text{Total Costs} - \text{Variable Costs}$$

$$FC = \$796{,}500 - (\$1.012 \times 629{,}600 \text{ Units})$$

$$FC = 796{,}500 - \$637{,}155 = \$159{,}345.$$

We have now "separated" the fixed costs from the variable costs. It isn't a perfect separation since only two points were used, the high and the low. With only two data points, we may question the accuracy of the result. Further, if a business has unusually wide swings in volume, the unusual operating conditions can skew the results.

CHAPTER 9

Least Squares Method

As explained in the previous chapter, when costs are neither purely variable nor purely fixed, we must identify and separate those variable and fixed components to be able to incorporate them into our cost-volume-profit analysis. The least squares method is a more precise mathematical approach to accomplish that objective. Let's expand on the example of Bob's Appliances. Over the past several years, Bob's volume of deliveries and delivery costs has varied from year to year as shown in Table 9.1, Deliveries and Costs.

Notice that the last 2 years contain the same data we used in the high-low method to determine the variable delivery cost per unit ($7.50) and the fixed delivery cost per year ($1,450).

To find the variable and fixed cost components of the delivery cost, follow these steps.[1]

Step 1: Enter your unit and cost data in a spreadsheet, as shown in Figure 9.1 (see columns B and C).

Step 2: To find the variable cost per delivery, enter the formula =linest(C4:C8,B4:B8). In Figure 9.1 this formula has been entered into cell B10.

In Figure 9.1, Calculating Variable Delivery Cost, the example spreadsheet gives the variable cost per delivery as $7.85.

Table 9.1. Deliveries and Costs

Year	Units delivered	Delivery costs
20AA	160	$2,700
20AB	170	$2,795
20AC	150	$2,610
20AD	140	$2,500
20AE	180	$2,800

◇	A	B	C
1		X	Y
2		Units	Delivery
3	Year	Delivered	Costs
4	20AA	160	$2,700
5	20AB	170	$2,795
6	20AC	150	$2,610
7	20AD	140	$2,500
8	20AE	180	$2,800
9			
10	linest	$7.85	
11			

Figure 9.1. Calculating Variable Delivery Cost

Step 3: To find the fixed delivery cost per year, enter the formula =intercept(C4:C8,B4:B8). In the Figure 9.2, Calculating Fixed Delivery Costs, this formula has been entered into cell B11. The example spreadsheet gives the fixed delivery cost as $1,425 per year.

◇	A	B	C
1		X	Y
2		Units	Delivery
3	Year	Delivered	Costs
4	20AA	160	$2,700
5	20AB	170	$2,795
6	20AC	150	$2,610
7	20AD	140	$2,500
8	20AE	180	$2,800
9			
10	linest	$7.85	
11	intercept	$1,425	
12			

Figure 9.2. Calculating Fixed Delivery Costs

Essentially, the spreadsheet is taking all the data (not just the highest and lowest values) and helping us find the fixed cost component (intercept) and the variable cost component (linest) from the following formula that we introduced in the last chapter:

$$Y = a + bX,$$

where

Y	=	Total (mixed) Costs of Delivery
a	=	Fixed Cost Component
b	=	Unit Variable Cost Component (Slope of the Line)
X	=	Number of Units Produced and Delivered.

This approach produces a mathematical estimate. But how precise is our estimate? To determine this we calculate a coefficient of determination.

Step 4: To find the coefficient of determination (often written R^2), enter the formula =RSQ(C4:C8,B4:B8). This formula has been entered into cell B12, shown in Figure 9.3, Calculating the Coefficient of Determination.

◇	A	B	C
1		X	Y
2		Units	Delivery
3	Year	Delivered	Costs
4	20AA	160	$2,700
5	20AB	170	$2,795
6	20AC	150	$2,610
7	20AD	140	$2,500
8	20AE	180	$2,800
9			
10	linest	$7.85	
11	intercept	$1,425	
12	R^2	0.94	
13			

Figure 9.3. Calculating the Coefficient of Determination

The example spreadsheet gives the coefficient of determination as 0.94. You may interpret the coefficient of determination as telling you that the changes in the volume of units delivered explain 94% of the changes in delivery costs incurred. Other changes in the business model not factored into this mathematical model explain only 6% of the changes in delivery costs. We conclude in this case that the values calculated for the variable and fixed cost components of delivery cost for Bob's Appliances are very good estimates of Bob's costs. Every company is different in terms of the changes that occur in the volume of units produced and sold and how these changes affect changes in costs.

Compare the results of the least squares method with the results of the high-low method discussed in the preceding chapter. This is shown in Table 9.2, Comparison of High-Low and Least Squares Results.

At the low volumes illustrated by Bob's Appliances, the difference between the two methods might be immaterial. However, at high volumes, the difference between the two methods could be substantial. The least squares method will produce the better estimates.

Why are the calculated values referred to as estimates when the spreadsheet process looks very precise? Let's select the most recent year, 20AE, and test the least squares values we calculated.

Total Variable Cost = $1,413 (180 Units × $7.85 per Unit)

Total Fixed Cost = $1,425

Total Costs = $2,838 Based on Least Squares Cost Estimates

We observe from the data that actual costs in year 20AE were $2,800, while the total costs calculated from our estimates are slightly different. This difference is a normal aspect of the mathematical process inherent in the least squares method.

You may be presented with daily, weekly, monthly, or quarterly data. You may have a large amount of data to work with. Unlike the high-low method of the preceding chapter, the least squares method considers all data available in

Table 9.2. Comparison of High-Low and Least Squares Results

Method	Variable costs	Fixed costs
High-low method	$7.50 per delivery	$1,450 per year
Least squares method	$7.85 per delivery	$1,425 per year

calculating the cost estimates. As with the high-low method, outliers (abnormal values) can distort the results.

As explained previously, one of the limiting assumptions is that there is no inflation or deflation to distort the results. Inflation or deflation tends to cause fixed costs to appear to be variable costs. The process of excluding the effect of inflation or deflation would be the same as for the high-low method.

Multiple regression, a more complex application of the least squares method, considers the effect on costs of several variables. Substantial business judgment and caution should be exercised in the selection of the variables. The multiple regression calculations can be performed with ease using statistics software such as SPSS. Application of multiple regression is beyond the scope of this book.

Using the Scattergraph

The scattergraph is a visual way to understand the coefficient of determination. Each data point is plotted on a graph. Then a line (called a trend line) is drawn to minimize the distances from the data points to the line. We do this to determine the "goodness of fit." Notice that all the data points are very near the trend line (a very good fit), which indicates a close relationship between changes in the number of units delivered and changes in the delivery costs.[2] An example of a scattergraph depicting a very good fit is shown in Figure 9.4, Scattergraph A.

In contrast, consider this next scattergraph shown in Figure 9.5, Scattergraph B. Notice that some of the data points do not lie very near the trend line. In fact, the point for 200 units delivered is quite far from the trend line. This off-the-line data point is called an outlier. There is an unusual cost-volume relationship in the year 20AH.[3] Also, contrast the first graph's R^2 value of 0.94, indicating a very close linear cost-volume relationship, with the second graph's R^2 value of only 0.74, indicating a less linear cost-volume relationship. This lower value of 0.74 would indicate that the variable and fixed cost estimates calculated are very rough (imprecise) estimates.

Finally, notice in Figure 9.6, Scattergraph C, how all remaining data points lie very near the trend line when the outlier is removed.[4] The R^2 value rises dramatically to 0.99, with no outlier data. The variable and fixed cost estimates calculated here are very good representatives of Bob's actual cost behavior.

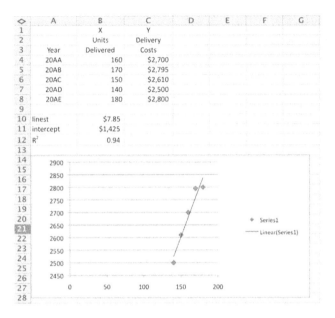

	A	B	C	D	E	F	G
1		X	Y				
2		Units	Delivery				
3	Year	Delivered	Costs				
4	20AA	160	$2,700				
5	20AB	170	$2,795				
6	20AC	150	$2,610				
7	20AD	140	$2,500				
8	20AE	180	$2,800				
9							
10	linest	$7.85					
11	intercept	$1,425					
12	R^2	0.94					

Figure 9.4. Scattergraph A

	A	B	C	D	E	F	G
1		X	Y				
2		Units	Delivery				
3	Year	Delivered	Costs				
4	20AF	195	$3,060				
5	20AG	225	$3,200				
6	20AH	200	$3,150				
7	20AI	208	$3,125				
8	20AJ	214	$3,160				
9							
10	linest	$3.77					
11	intercept	$2,353					
12	R^2	0.74					

Figure 9.5. Scattergraph B

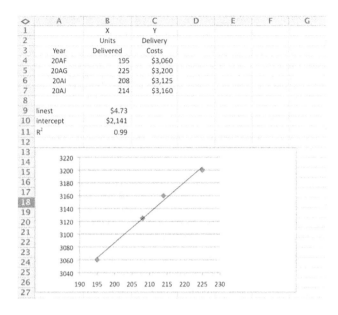

Figure 9.6. Scattergraph C

CHAPTER 10

Changing Costs

Our friend Bob, with whom we are getting quite well acquainted by now, is experiencing rising costs for the appliances he sells. He is wondering how this change will affect his breakeven point. Table 10.1, Refrigerator Contribution Margin, represents a typical refrigerator sale for Bob.

Here is Bob's breakeven point before the change in cost:

$$\frac{\$437,500 \text{ Annual Fixed Costs}}{\$350 \text{ CM}} = \begin{array}{l} 1,250 \text{ Total Units to} \\ \text{Be Sold Annually.} \end{array}$$

This translates into $1,250,000 sales ($1,000 per unit × 1,250 refrigerators) needed to break even.

Recently, the manufacturer notified Bob that his cost to purchase a refrigerator would go up from $650 to $700. Assume that local competition will not allow Bob to increase the selling price of his refrigerators. Now, the typical refrigerator sale looks like the information portrayed in Table 10.2, Contribution Margin With Cost Inflation.

Here is Bob's breakeven point after the change in cost:

$$\frac{\$437,500 \text{ Annual Fixed Costs}}{\$300 \text{ CM}} = \begin{array}{l} 1,459 \text{ Total Units to} \\ \text{Be Sold Annually.} \end{array}$$

Table 10.1. Refrigerator Contribution Margin

Selling price to the customer	$1,000	100%
Bob's purchase cost	$650	65%
Bob's contribution margin (CM)	$350	35% contribution margin ratio

Table 10.2. Contribution Margin With Cost Inflation

Selling price to the customer	$1,000	100%
Bob's purchase cost	$700	70%
Bob's contribution margin	$300	30% contribution margin ratio

This translates into $1,459,000 sales ($1,000 × 1,459 refrigerators) needed to break even.

Now, let's change the scenario. Assume local competition will allow Bob to increase the selling price of refrigerators to reflect his increased cost. Bob may want to keep the contribution margin amount per refrigerator constant. In that event, his new breakeven calculation is shown in Table 10.3, Contribution Margin With New Selling Price.

Here is Bob's breakeven point after the changes in cost and selling price:

$$\frac{\$437{,}500\ \text{Annual Fixed Costs}}{\$350\ \text{CM}} = \begin{array}{l} 1{,}250\ \text{Total Units to Be} \\ \text{Sold Annually.} \end{array}$$

Amazingly, Bob's breakeven point in units to be sold is unchanged from his original numbers, before the cost increased. However, he must sell $1,312,500 (instead of $1,250,000) to break even.

Bob might, instead, want to earn the same contribution margin ratio on his sales. His new breakeven calculation can be obtained from the data shown in Table 10.4, Target Contribution Margin Ratio.

Here is Bob's breakeven point after the change in cost:

$$\frac{\$437{,}500\ \text{Annual Fixed Costs}}{\$377\ \text{CM}} = \begin{array}{l} 1{,}161\ \text{Total Units to} \\ \text{Be Sold Annually.} \end{array}$$

Remarkably, Bob can break even by selling *fewer* refrigerators after the cost increase when he holds his contribution margin ratio unchanged.

Table 10.3. Contribution Margin With New Selling Price

Selling price to the customer	$1,050	100%
Bob's purchase cost	$700	66.67%
Bob's contribution margin	$350	33.33% contribution margin ratio

Table 10.4. Target Contribution Margin Ratio

Selling price to the customer	$1,077	100% ($700 ÷ 0.65)
Bob's purchase cost	$700	65%
Bob's contribution margin	$377	35% target contribution margin ratio

Changing the Variable Costs of Manufacturing

A retailer like Bob has one way to deal with the decision of what to do as costs change. Changing variable costs creates a similar challenge for manufacturing firms whose managers need to know the impact of such changes on the breakeven point. Sometimes without warning suppliers will take an action that has an immediate, direct effect on the unit variable cost. While they can lower their prices, it is the increase in costs of input factors that will be the dominant concern when considering the impact of such changes on the breakeven point.

The application of breakeven analysis reviewed here seeks to answer a simple question: "How would a change in variable cost affect the sales goals to generate equal or better profit?" This application of breakeven analysis takes as a given that the current level of profit is acceptable to managers. Fixed costs and selling price are assumed to remain unchanged.

The application is built on the change in contribution margin that a change in variable costs represents.

More specifically, a formula provided by Smith and Nagle[1] is helpful:

% Change in Sales Volume Needed = −Change in Contribution Margin ÷ (Contribution Margin + Change in Contribution Margin).

Using algebra notation we can simplify this with the following:

$$\%\Delta \text{ Sales} = -\Delta CM \div (CM + \Delta CM),$$

where

%Δ Sales = % Change in Sales Units Needed to Generate Equal Profit

ΔCM = Change in Contribution Margin (Measured in Dollars)

CM = Contribution Margin (in Dollars).

Assuming that fixed costs or selling price does not change as a result of the change in variable costs, this formula calculates the minimum percent change in sales volume at the *new* variable cost needed to generate the same level of profit. But variable costs can go *up* or *down*. When variable costs go down, generally this relieves some of the pressure to achieve the sales volume required to achieve desired profit. When variable costs go up, it puts additional pressure on sales volume to achieve desired profit. It is an increase in variable costs that we will most often be concerned about.

Increases in variable costs can come from many places, such as new marketing ideas like product packaging, product design changes, or product style changes. Another source of change is when suppliers of components and materials raise their prices.

To see how this simple formula works, consider the following example.

Heartland Machine, Inc.

Heartland Machine, Inc., sells 10,000 specially designed machine tools annually for total global sales revenue of $14,000,000. That's $1,400 per unit selling price. The marketing manager proposed using new, more expensive packaging that would cost $45 per unit. In effect, this change would raise the unit variable cost by 4.09%. He argued that better packaging would give distributors an advantage in selling the machine tools to their customers. Packaging is an important signal to customers of the value they are getting. The logic was that if distributors promoted the product more because of the exciting packaging, Heartland would sell more machine tools and generate more revenue and more profit.

The general manager was not immediately convinced. He said, "Fine. But before we implement new product packaging, I need to know the impact on sales that we need to see in order to maintain or improve upon current profit."

Unit Variable Costs for the Heartland Machine tool equal $1,010 per unit. Subtracting the unit variable cost from the unit selling price of $1,400 reveals the unit contribution margin of $390. This assumes that the selling price will remain unchanged.

The *minimum* percent increase in sales volume needed to maintain the same level of profit after the increase to variable costs is as follows:

$$
\begin{aligned}
\%\Delta \text{ Sales Units} \ &= \ -\Delta CM \div (CM + \Delta CM) \\
&= \ -(-45) \div (390 - 45) \\
&= \ 45 \div (345) \\
&= \ 13.04\%
\end{aligned}
$$

In this case a 13% increase in sales volume is needed to maintain the same level of profit after the addition of new packaging. The sales manager might have an opinion regarding the likelihood of achieving this.

The results of this shorthand method can be confirmed using the traditional breakeven analysis formula as shown in Table 10.5, Changing Variable Costs at Heartland Machine, where breakeven point in units (BE_U) equals fixed costs (FC) divided by the contribution margin (CM), or $BE_U = FC \div CM$.

Impact of Changing Fixed Costs

Adding fixed costs to an organization is sometimes necessary for the organization to continue carrying out its mission. A manager may need to be added. Extra employees may be needed in the assembly line or packing and shipping department. Customer service may need more trained staff. Sales personnel may need to be hired and trained. Additional money may need to be spent on advertising to stimulate demand. What is common to all these additions to fixed cost is that the contribution margin must "carry" a heavier weight than before. This means that the volume of sales needed to break even increases.

Calculating the impact from a change in fixed costs on profit is straightforward using the following formula: % Change in Sales Units Needed = % Change in Fixed Costs:

$$\%\Delta \text{ Sales} = \%\Delta \text{ FC},$$

Table 10.5. Changing Variable Costs at Heartland Machine

	Before	After	Change	% Change
Fixed costs	$3,900,000	$3,900,000	0	0.00%
Variable costs	$1,010	$1,055	45	4.46%
Selling price	$1,400	$1,400	0	0.00%
Contribution margin	$390	$345	−45	11.5%
Breakeven units	$10,000	$11,304	1,304	13.04%

where

%Δ Sales = % Change in Sales Units Needed to Generate Equal Profit

%Δ FC = % Change in Fixed Costs.

Assuming that variable costs and selling price do not change as a result of the change in fixed costs, this formula calculates the minimum percent change in *sales* volume that the company would have to generate to cover the incremental fixed costs that are incurred.

To see how this simple formula works, consider the following example. Instead of changing its packaging, let's say Heartland managers decide to hire more sales personnel and give them training to sell the machine tools to distributors worldwide. The sales manager estimates this will add $400,000 annually to the company's fixed costs. For this example, selling price and variable costs will remain unchanged, meaning that the contribution margin is unchanged.

To determine the impact of increasing fixed costs, the calculation is straightforward as follows:

$$\%\Delta \text{ Sales Units } = \%\Delta \text{ FC}$$
$$= 10.26\%$$

We can see this illustrated in Table 10.6, Changing Fixed Costs at Heartland Machine.

In the table we can see that fixed costs increase by 10.26%. The new breakeven volume is exactly 10.26% greater after the change in fixed costs. In this case, if Heartland Machine adds $400,000 of fixed costs, 1,026 additional units must be sold to justify the additional costs.

Table 10.6. Changing Fixed Costs at Heartland Machine

	Before	After	Change	% Change
Fixed costs	$3,900,000	$4,300,000	400,000	10.26%
Variable costs	$1,010	$1,010	0	0.00%
Selling price	$1,400	$1,400	0	0.00%
Contribution margin	$390	$390	0	0.00%
Breakeven units	$10,000	$11,026	1,026	10.26%

We should recognize that in real life fixed costs may be changing at the same time as changes taking place in the contribution margin. The natural desire is, if possible, to maintain current profit margins even under changing conditions. Accordingly, the natural question to ask is this: In order to maintain current profit margin, what is the percentage change in sales volume needed when fixed costs change by a known percentage and at the same time the contribution margin changes by a known percentage?

The answer to this question can be found by using in the following formula:

$$[(1 + \%\Delta F) / (1 + \%\Delta C)] - 1$$

Where:

F = Fixed Costs in $

C = Contribution Margin (%)

%Δ = the percentage change

Following John Tse's[1] lead and using the formula above we offer a generic quick-use table that helps a manager to estimate at-a-glance the impact of changing (increasing) fixed costs and changing (increasing) contribution margin. This is shown in Table 10.7.

Some interesting observations can be made by viewing Table 10.7. First, the obvious finding is that when the percent change in fixed costs equals the percent change in contribution margin, the percent increase in sales volume needed to maintain current profit is always zero. This is evident from the formula.

Second, an interesting mirror image occurs in the table showing that for every five percentage-point difference between the change in fixed costs and the change in contribution margin the absolute value of change in sales volume needed is identical. Also, for every 10 percentage-point difference between the change in fixed costs and the change in contribution margin the absolute change in sales volume needed is identical. These mirror images are identified with shaded cells in the table. For example, notice that when the percent change in fixed costs is 5% and the change in contribution margin is 10%, the change in sales volume

Table 10.7. Fixed Costs Increasing and Contribution Margin Increasing

% Δ in Sales Volume Needed to Maintain Current Profit

WHEN %ΔFC =	WHEN %ΔCM =							
	1.0%	3.0%	5.0%	10.0%	15.0%	20.0%	25.0%	30.0%
1.0%	0.00%	-1.94%	-3.81%	-8.18%	-12.17%	-15.83%	-19.20%	-22.31%
3.0%	1.98%	0.00%	-1.90%	-6.36%	-10.43%	-14.17%	-17.60%	-20.77%
5.0%	3.96%	1.94%	0.00%	-4.55%	-8.70%	-12.50%	-16.00%	-19.23%
7.0%	5.94%	3.88%	1.90%	-2.73%	-6.96%	-10.83%	-14.40%	-17.69%
10.0%	8.91%	6.80%	4.76%	0.00%	-4.35%	-8.33%	-12.00%	-15.38%
12.0%	10.89%	8.74%	6.67%	1.82%	-2.61%	-6.67%	-10.40%	-13.85%
15.0%	13.86%	11.65%	9.52%	4.55%	0.00%	-4.17%	-8.00%	-11.54%
17.0%	15.84%	13.59%	11.43%	6.36%	1.74%	-2.50%	-6.40%	-10.00%
20.0%	18.81%	16.50%	14.29%	9.09%	4.35%	0.00%	-4.00%	-7.69%
22.0%	20.79%	18.45%	16.19%	10.91%	6.09%	1.67%	-2.40%	-6.15%
25.0%	23.76%	21.36%	19.05%	13.64%	8.70%	4.17%	0.00%	-3.85%
27.0%	25.74%	23.30%	20.95%	15.45%	10.43%	5.83%	1.60%	-2.31%
30.0%	28.71%	26.21%	23.81%	18.18%	13.04%	8.33%	4.00%	0.00%

needed to maintain profit is –4.55%. And when the change in fixed cost is 15% and the change in contribution margin is 10% (still a difference of 5 points), the change in sales volume needed to maintain profit is +4.55%. Also, in Table 10.7 when the change in fixed costs is 5% but the change in contribution margin is 15%, the percent change in sales volume needed to achieve the same level of profit is –8.70%. And, when the change in fixed costs is 25% but the change in contribution margin is 15% (still 10 percentage-points different), the percent change in sales volume needed to maintain current profit is +8.70%. The absolute values of these two are identical.

Third, when the change in contribution margin reaches 25%, for every additional 5% change in fixed costs, the change in sales volume needed to maintain profit improves by 25%. (See the column 25% change in contribution margin.)

When contribution margin increases, this is favorable. But contribution margin can change in an unfavorable direction, too, as prices are squeezed and variable costs inflate. As fixed costs increase and contribution margin *decreases*, the company faces the most challenges. Using the formula, we offer the quick-use table shown in Table 10.8 to help the busy manager estimate the impact on sales volume under these conditions in order to maintain current profit.

Something obvious to managers from Table 10.8 is that under conditions of declining market prices or increasing variable costs (i.e., supplier prices) such that the contribution margin decreases, a company that expands its fixed costs must consider ways to counteract the change in contribution margin.

Another observation is that the percent increase in sales volume needed is always more than the sum of the percent increase in fixed costs and the absolute value of the percent change in contribution margin. For example, when the change in fixed costs is 10% and the change in contribution margin is –5% (an absolute value of 5), the increase in sales volume needed to maintain current profit is 15.79%. When the change in fixed costs is 17% and the change in contribution margin is –10% (an absolute value of 10), the increase in sales volume needed to maintain current profit is 30%.

Table 10.8. Fixed Costs Increasing and Contribution Margin Decreasing

% Δ in Sales Volume Needed to Maintain Current Profit

WHEN %ΔFC =	WHEN %ΔCM =							
	-1.0%	-3.0%	-5.0%	-10.0%	-15.0%	-20.0%	-25.0%	-30.0%
1.0%	2.02%	4.12%	6.32%	12.22%	18.82%	26.25%	34.67%	44.29%
3.0%	4.04%	6.19%	8.42%	14.44%	21.18%	28.75%	37.33%	47.14%
5.0%	6.06%	8.25%	10.53%	16.67%	23.53%	31.25%	40.00%	50.00%
7.0%	8.08%	10.31%	12.63%	18.89%	25.88%	33.75%	42.67%	52.86%
10.0%	11.11%	13.40%	15.79%	22.22%	29.41%	37.50%	46.67%	57.14%
12.0%	13.13%	15.46%	17.89%	24.44%	31.76%	40.00%	49.33%	60.00%
15.0%	16.16%	18.56%	21.05%	27.78%	35.29%	43.75%	53.33%	64.29%
17.0%	18.18%	20.62%	23.16%	30.00%	37.65%	46.25%	56.00%	67.14%
20.0%	21.21%	23.71%	26.32%	33.33%	41.18%	50.00%	60.00%	71.43%
22.0%	23.23%	25.77%	28.42%	35.56%	43.53%	52.50%	62.67%	74.29%
25.0%	26.26%	28.87%	31.58%	38.89%	47.06%	56.25%	66.67%	78.57%
27.0%	28.28%	30.93%	33.68%	41.11%	49.41%	58.75%	69.33%	81.43%
30.0%	31.31%	34.02%	36.84%	44.44%	52.94%	62.50%	73.33%	85.71%

CHAPTER 11

Changing Prices

Costs are not the only item that can change, making the work of a manager challenging. Companies can go along quite comfortably for weeks or months on track to achieve their annual profit goals. Sometimes without warning, competitors take an action or customers begin to change their tastes, requiring managers to consider changing selling price.

The application of breakeven analysis reviewed here seeks to answer this simple question: How would a selling price change affect sales goals and still generate equal or better profit?

This application of breakeven analysis takes as a given that the current level of profit is acceptable to managers. The application is built on the ratio of the change in selling price to contribution margin. Fixed costs and variable costs are assumed to remain unchanged in the short run. To help us with this situation, Smith and Nagle[1] offer a useful formula to find the answer:

% Change in Sales Volume Needed = −Change in Price ÷ (Contribution Margin + Change in Price).

Using algebra notation we can simplify this with the following:

$$\%\Delta \text{ Sales} = -\Delta P \div (CM + \Delta P),$$

where

%Δ Sales = % Change in Sales Volume Needed to Generate Equal Profit

ΔP = Change in Price (Measured in Dollars)

CM = Contribution Margin (in Dollars).

Assuming the variable costs do not change as a result of the price change, this formula calculates the minimum percent change in sales volume at the *new* price needed to generate the same level of profit. But price can go *up* or *down*. When price goes down, the worry is whether enough sales volume will be generated to achieve the desired profit. When price goes up, the worry becomes whether too many customers will go away to achieve the desired profit.

Recall from economic theory that price *decreases* are expected to result in a percent increase in sales volume. Thus, under conditions of a proposed price reduction, the formula shows the minimum percent increase in sales needed to achieve the current profit.

Price *increases* are expected to result in a percent decrease in sales volume. But in many cases the precise responsiveness of customers is not known. Thus, the formula shows the maximum percent decrease in sales that can be tolerated and still generate the same level of profit that the company enjoys before the price change. Managers are required to make a judgment regarding the likelihood of the decrease in sales occurring as a result of a price change.

Example 1

Olympia Vacuum, Inc., sells 400,000 vacuum cleaners annually for total sales revenue of $24,000,000. That's $60 per vacuum. Because sales were beginning to slow compared with this time last year, the marketing manager proposed decreasing the price by 5% from $60 to $57 per unit. The proposed change in price is just $3. He argued that this would give retailers the opportunity to either keep the retail price the same or decrease the price to capture more sales. The general manager said, "Fine. But before we implement the new price policy, I need to know the impact on sales that we should expect."

$$\text{Unit Variable Costs} = \$40 \text{ per Vacuum}$$
$$\text{Contribution Margin} = (\$60 - \$40) = \$20$$

The *minimum* percent increase in sales volume needed to maintain the same level of profit after the 5% price reduction is as follows:

$$
\begin{aligned}
\%\Delta \text{ Sales Volume Needed} \ &= \ -\Delta P \ / \ (CM + \Delta P) \\
&= \ 3/(20 - 3) \\
&= \ 3/17 \\
&= \ 17.65\%
\end{aligned}
$$

In this case a little over 17% increase in sales volume is needed to maintain the same level of profit after the price reduction.

Example 2

Eagle Cap Wilderness Bikes sells 2,000 high-impact elite racing mountain bicycles for total sales revenue of $19,000,000. There is so much demand for the bikes that the marketing manager recommends to the general manager that the price be *increased* by 15%. She argues that the scarcity of the bikes coupled with the increase in price would strengthen the brand's power with elite riders who seek a competitive edge and who are willing to pay almost any reasonable price for this advantage. The general manager of Eagle Cap says, "Let's say that what you assume is correct regarding customer price sensitivities. Though frankly I doubt customers are *that* insensitive to a price increase. Don't forget there are other really good race-quality mountain bikes on the market. And don't confuse a spike in customer interest with normal interest through the rest of the year. Before we implement the new price policy, I need to know the impact on sales that we should expect. Specifically, what percent change in sales volume can we tolerate on the off-chance that sales decline with the price increase."

Unit variable costs for these ultra lightweight but durable bikes equal $3,450. Unit selling price is $9,500. This makes the contribution margin a hefty $6,050—potentially a high-profitability product.

Since the marketing manager is proposing a price increase, normally we should expect a *decrease* in sales volume (unless this particular product is truly creating customers who are less responsive to price changes). The *maximum* change in sales that Eagle Cap Wilderness Bikes can tolerate with the price increase of 15% is as follows:

$$\%\Delta \text{ Sales Volume Tolerated} = -\Delta P / (CM + \Delta P)$$
$$= -\$1,425 / (\$6,050 + \$1,425)$$
$$= -19.06\%$$

Changing prices also affect services. For example, the Red River Padres minor league baseball team sells tickets to its home games at $6 each. The stadium seats 1,500 fans. At the typical home game the ballpark is at 80% of capacity. The owner of the team estimates that the team incurs

$0.95 in variable costs at each home game. This leaves a contribution margin of $5.05 on each ticket sold. The Padres' publicity manager suggests to the owner that the team should consider a special promotion by selling tickets at just $4 for one home game to see if this will pump up attendance.

The owner asks how many additional tickets need to be sold if the price is reduced for the special event. Because of the price reduction, contribution margin for each ticket will drop to $3.05 per ticket sold.

The minimum additional ticket sales needed to maintain the same level of profit after the price decrease are as follows:

$$
\begin{aligned}
\%\Delta \text{ Sales Needed} \quad &= \quad -\Delta P \ / \ (\text{CM} + \Delta P) \\
&= \quad -(-\$2) \div (\$5.05 - \$2) \\
&= \quad \$2 \div \$3.05 \\
&= \quad 65.57\%
\end{aligned}
$$

Rounding this, we might say under the conditions proposed by the publicity manager a 66% increase in ticket sales will be needed to achieve the current level of profit.

While the owner was calculating this figure, the publicity manager also suggested that every fan attending the special promotional game be given a sparkler firework valued at $0.25. These fireworks would be used after the game in center field as part of the fireworks extravaganza.

Upon hearing this additional detail, the owner continued calculating. When he was finished, he looked up and simply said, "Are you crazy? If we cut the price but do not give away sparklers, we will need at least a 66% increase in attendance to achieve our current per-game profit. But if we then increase the variable costs by 25 cents to put a sparkler in every ticket holder's hot little hand, we'd need to add another 5.2% to the number of tickets sold to maintain our profit. This would put required attendance over the maximum available capacity by well over 500 ticket holders. What I'd like to know is where are you are going to put these 500+ people who don't have seats so we can make our profit? Are they supposed to bring their own chairs?"

An Alternative Approach and a Useful Table

Former Purdue University professor John Tse[2] offered an alternative approach to solving this problem. When a price reduction is contemplated, such as when managers want to stimulate increased demand for products, someone needs to sell more units of the product in order to achieve the same profit level.

Tse's formula is as follows:

$$\Delta V\% = [\Delta s\% \div ((100 - v\%s1) - \Delta s\%)] \times 100,$$

where

$$\Delta V\% = \text{Minimum Increase in Sales Volume (Expressed as Percentage of Breakeven Sales Volume Before Price Change)}$$

$$S1 = \text{Selling Price Before Price Reduction}$$

$$\Delta s\% = \text{Reduction in Selling Price (Expressed as Percentage of Selling Price Before Price Reduction)}$$

$$v\%s1 = \text{Variable Cost (Expressed as Percentage of Selling Price Before Price Reduction).}$$

Example 3

To use our previous example, Olympia Vacuum, Inc., is making a profit by selling its vacuums at $60 per unit. The sales director recommends a 30% reduction in selling price in order to be competitive in the market. The chief financial officer wants to know what percent additional sales volume will be needed to maintain the company's current profit. Assume that the unit variable cost is 33.3% of the current selling price. If we also assume that everything else will remain unchanged in the company's cost structure, we can use Tse's formula to calculate the answer as follows:

$$\Delta V\% = [30 \div ((100 - 33.33) - 30)] \times 100$$

$$\Delta V\% = 82\%.$$

This means that if the price is reduced by 30%, the sales team will need to generate an increase of 82% of current sales volume. If the current volume that generates the desired profit is 75,000 units, the new sales volume will be

$$75,000 \times 1.82 = 136,000 \text{ Units.}$$

Changing Prices and Variable Costs

But changing price is sometimes accompanied by changes in unit variable costs. Using his formula, Tse presented a useful table that allows a manager at a glance to estimate the percent change in sales volume needed to achieve current level of profits when both selling price (reduction) and unit variable costs (increase) change in an unfavorable direction. Tse published his table decades ago, but it has gotten lost in the shuffle of advancing knowledge. We reproduce it here to help the busy manager (see Table 11.1).

One other type of change that should be considered is the prospect that fixed costs also change. When these change, there is an immediate impact on the breakeven point. To this we turn next.

Table 11.1. Adapted From Tse's Table for Finding the Minimum Increase of Sales Volume Required to Accompany Selected Price Reductions to Maintain the Profit Position Before Price Reduction Under Selected Cost-Price Structures

Percent increase in sales required to maintain current profit

% PRICE CHANGE	VARIABLE COSTS AS % OF SELLING PRICE BEFORE PRICE REDUCTION								
	10.00	20.00	30.00	40.00	50.00	60.00	70.00	80.00	90.00
1.00	1.12%	1.27%	1.45%	1.69%	2.04%	2.56%	3.45%	5.26%	11.11%
3.00	3.45%	3.90%	4.48%	5.26%	6.38%	8.11%	11.11%	17.65%	42.86%
5.00	5.88%	6.67%	7.69%	9.09%	11.11%	14.29%	20.00%	33.33%	100.00%
7.00	8.43%	9.59%	11.11%	13.21%	16.28%	21.21%	30.43%	53.85%	233.33%
10.00	12.50%	14.29%	16.67%	20.00%	25.00%	33.33%	50.00%	100.00%	Loss*
15.00	20.00%	23.08%	27.27%	33.33%	42.86%	60.00%	100.00%	300.00%	
17.00	23.29%	26.98%	32.08%	39.53%	51.52%	73.91%	130.77%	566.67%	
20.00	28.57%	33.33%	40.00%	50.00%	66.67%	100.00%	200.00%	Loss	
25.00	38.46%	45.45%	55.56%	71.43%	100.00%	166.67%	500.00%		
27.00	42.86%	50.94%	62.79%	81.82%	117.39%	207.69%	900.00%		
30.00	50.00%	60.00%	75.00%	100.00%	150.00%	300.00%	Loss		
33.00	57.89%	70.21%	89.19%	122.22%	194.12%	471.43%			
35.00	63.64%	77.78%	100.00%	140.00%	233.33%	700.00%			
36.00	66.67%	81.82%	105.88%	150.00%	257.14%	900.00%			

Table 11.1. Adapted From Tse's Table for Finding the Minimum Increase of Sales Volume Required to Accompany Selected Price Reductions to Maintain the Profit Position Before Price Reduction Under Selected Cost-Price Structures (continued)

| | Percent increase in sales required to maintain current profit | | | | | | | | |
| | VARIABLE COSTS AS % OF SELLING PRICE BEFORE PRICE REDUCTION | | | | | | | | |
% PRICE CHANGE	10.00	20.00	30.00	40.00	50.00	60.00	70.00	80.00	90.00
40.00	80.00%	100.00%	133.33%	200.00%	400.00%	Loss			
45.00	100.00%	128.57%	180.00%	300.00%	900.00%				
50.00	125.00%	166.67%	250.00%	500.00%	Loss				
54.00	150.00%	207.69%	337.50%	900.00%					
55.00	157.14%	220.00%	366.67%	1100.00%					
60.00	200.00%	300.00%	600.00%	Loss					
63.00	233.33%	370.59%	900.00%						
65.00	260.00%	433.33%	1300.00%						
66.00	275.00%	471.43%	1650.00%						

Table 11.1. Adapted From Tse's Table for Finding the Minimum Increase of Sales Volume Required to Accompany Selected Price Reductions to Maintain the Profit Position Before Price Reduction Under Selected Cost-Price Structures (continued)

% PRICE CHANGE	Percent increase in sales required to maintain current profit								
	VARIABLE COSTS AS % OF SELLING PRICE BEFORE PRICE REDUCTION								
	10.00	20.00	30.00	40.00	50.00	60.00	70.00	80.00	90.00
70.00	350.00%	700.00%	Loss						
72.00	400.00%	900.00%							
75.00	500.00%	1500.00%							
80.00	800.00%	Loss							
81.00	900.00%								
85.00	1700.00%								
90.00	Loss								

*Loss means that the selling price dropped below the variable cost, causing a loss on the sale of every unit.

When this occurs, you cannot "make up the difference" by selling more! The more you sell, the more you lose.

Source. Tse, John Y. D. (1960). *Profit planning through volume-cost analysis.* New York: Macmillan. p. 83. Used with permission.

CHAPTER 12

Selling Price at Various Volumes

Bob, the appliance retailer, recently saw an ad for a competitor appliance store. The competitor was offering to sell a refrigerator for substantially less than Bob's price. Bob wondered, "We are selling identical refrigerators. How can they sell them for so much less and still make a profit?"

Assume Bob's Appliances sells only refrigerators (a simplifying assumption). We have the information shown in Table 12.1, Impact of Changing Volume.

To answer Bob's question, there are three changes that would allow a lower selling price:

1. As shown in Table 12.1, selling a larger volume of units would spread the fixed costs over more units and reduce the fixed cost per unit.
2. Total fixed costs could be reduced, which would reduce the fixed cost per unit. Suggestions for reducing total fixed costs could include reduced rent (a less expensive store or a smaller store), becoming more energy efficient, and shopping for a lower premium on business insurance.
3. Accepting a lower desired profit would allow Bob to reduce his selling price.

Next, let's consider a different business environment and the management concept of target costing.

Have you ever wondered how the price of a product can drop dramatically after the product has been on the market for a while? The videocassette recorder (VCR), introduced to consumers around 1980, sold for about $1,000. Twenty years later, a VCR sold for perhaps 10% of

Table 12.1. Impact of Changing Volume

Annual volume of refrigerators sold	500	1,000	1,500
Annual fixed costs (FC)	$437,500	$437,500	$437,500
Annual desired profit (DP)	$100,000	$100,000	$100,000
Total contribution margin (CM = FC + DP)	$537,500	$537,500	$537,500
Annual sales volume (units) (SU)	÷ 500	÷ 1,000	÷ 1,500
Contribution margin per unit (CMU = CM ÷ SU)	$1,075	$537.50	$358.33
Variable cost per unit (VCU)	$650	$650	$650
Selling price per unit (SPU = CMU + VCU)	= $1,725	= $1,187.50	= $1,008.33

the original 1980 selling price. There are a number of reasons, but we will focus on two: (a) the increase in the quantity of units sold and (b) the reduction of variable costs per unit. Assume the data in Table 12.2, Impact of Changing Volume and Variable Costs.

Between 1980 and 2000, two obvious things happened. First, the sales demand increased greatly. That allowed the producer to spread the fixed costs and desired profit over many more units and reduced the contribution margin needed per unit from $400 in 1980 to only $30 in 2000. The hefty reduction in total required contribution margin allowed the producer to significantly reduce the per-unit selling price while continuing to earn the same total profits.

Second, the variable cost per unit declined dramatically, from $600 per unit in 1980 to $70 per unit in 2000. This cost reduction may be

Table 12.2. Impact of Changing Volume and Variable Costs

Year	1980	2000
Annual fixed costs (FC)	$5,000,000	$5,000,000
Annual desired profit (DP)	$1,000,000	$1,000,000
Total contribution margin (CM = FC + DP)	$6,000,000	$6,000,000
Sales demand (units) (SU)	÷ 15,000	÷ 200,000
Contribution margin per unit (CMU = CM ÷ SU)	$400	$30
Variable cost per unit (VCU)	$600	$70
Selling price per unit (SPU = CMU + VCU)	= $1,000	= $100

credited to cheaper materials, low-cost labor in third-world countries, and innovations in the production process. But these cost reductions were driven by a shift in management thinking. Traditional cost-plus pricing (illustrated in the 1980 VCR example) accumulated all costs, added a desired profit, and magically arrived at the "right" selling price.

Target costing is a reversal of the thinking in traditional cost-plus price setting. Target costing first determines through market research an appropriate selling price per unit and volume of units that can likely be sold. Management then sets the desired profit (per unit or in total). Finally, the difference between the selling price and the desired profit is the cost the company can afford to spend to produce and sell the product. At this point, engineers from research and development and personnel from materials acquisition, human resources, and production team up to find a way to make the product at or below the target cost.[1]

CHAPTER 13

Multiple Breakeven Points

Because of unpredictable student enrollment, the local community college leases classroom space and hires adjunct professors to teach multiple sections of introductory English and mathematics courses. The college requires that each course section taught have a minimum of 6 and a maximum of 25 students.

The scenario in the preceding paragraph introduces the interesting possibility that an organization may break even at more than one volume of sales. Whenever an organization's fixed costs change, the breakeven point changes. Fixed costs, in the community college example, would be classroom leases and adjunct professor salaries. For the college, the relationship is a circular one. If more students enroll, the college must hire more adjunct professors. If the college hires more adjunct professors, its fixed costs and its breakeven point rise, requiring more students to enroll. Observe in the following example how the breakeven point moves upward as student enrollment increases.

Assume the following data shown in Table 13.1, Community College Selected Costs and Prices.

One section taught will be the unit of measure. We need to calculate the contribution margin per section taught. Each section will be filled to its maximum of 25 students before another section is offered.

Table 13.1. Community College Selected Costs and Prices

Student tuition per course	$120
Instructional supplies per student per course	$20
Adjunct professor salary per course section taught	$2,100
Leased building for eight classrooms per semester	$2,000

Tuition Revenue per Section = ($120 × 25 Students) = $3,000

Variable Costs for Instructional Supplies per Section =
($20 × 25 Students) = $500

Variable Cost of Professor's Salary per Section = $2,100

Contribution Margin per Section = ($3,000 − $500 − $2,100) = $400

Let's calculate the breakeven point:

$$\frac{\$2,000 \text{ Fixed Cost (Lease)}}{\$400 \text{ per Section Contribution Margin}} = \text{5 Units (Sections to Be Taught).}$$

The community college must have five sections filled with the maximum number of students to reach breakeven.

Now, let's consider the surprising results of different numbers of students enrolling shown in Table 13.2, Profit and (Loss) at Different Enrollments.

How can it be that the college breaks even at two points (125 students enrolled *and* 167 students enrolled), while it earns a profit with only 147 students enrolled, but loses money with 157 students enrolled? The answer lies in the concept of the relevant range. Every time student enrollment exceeds the maximum of 25 students per classroom, enrollment exceeds the relevant range, so capacity must increase (an additional professor must be hired to teach an additional section). This increase in

Table 13.2. Profit and (Loss) at Different Enrollments

Student enrollment	125	147	157	167
Course sections	5	6	7	7
Tuition revenue	$15,000	$17,640	$18,840	$20,040
Variable cost supplies	$2,500	$2,940	$3,140	$3,340
Salaries	$10,500	$12,600	$14,700	$14,700
Lease	$2,000	$2,000	$2,000	$2,000
Profit (Loss)	$0	$100	($1,000)	$0

capacity increases the fixed costs incurred and, consequently, changes the breakeven point. Let's calculate the breakeven student enrollment for six sections taught.

$$\frac{\$14,600 \text{ Fixed Costs (Salaries + Lease)}}{\$100 \text{ per Student Contribution Margin}} = 146 \text{ Students}$$

Recalling that initial breakeven was at five sections, if the college decides to open a sixth section, it needs to be reasonably sure of obtaining between 146 and 150 students to cover all its costs. If student enrollment rises above 150 students, the college must open a seventh section.

If the college offers seven course sections, the breakeven point would be

$$\frac{\$16,700 \text{ Fixed Costs (Salaries + Lease)}}{\$100 \text{ per Student Contribution Margin}} = 167 \text{ Students.}$$

If potential enrollment exceeds 150 students, so that a seventh section is needed, the college needs to attract at least 167 students to cover all its costs.

The preceding example has illustrated multiple breakeven points when sales volume rises. The same concepts and methods apply when sales volume declines if the organization is able to reduce its capacity (fixed costs). In the college or university environment, if the additional professors hired were tenured professors instead of adjunct professors, then the educational institution would not be able to reduce its fixed costs and, therefore, would not be able to reduce its breakeven point.

Readers who are interested in a more mathematical approach to analyzing business scenarios with multiple breakeven points are referred to the discussion of the quadratic equation in chapter 15.

CHAPTER 14

Net Present Value Method

Net present value (NPV) is one of a group of topics often referred to as capital budgeting. It isn't often viewed as a cost-volume-profit technique. In this method, we will calculate a cost or a value, which we will call the *indifference point*. Typically, an organization is faced with deciding between two alternatives, each of which will have the same result to the organization (hence, the indifference). Sometimes, one application of this method is called the *outsource decision* (or the make-or-buy decision).

Let's get started with an example.

Example 1

Statewide Industries currently has a landscaping department to care for the vast, tastefully decorated grounds surrounding its office and laboratory complex. Statewide has just received a proposal from a landscaping contractor that, if accepted, would outsource the landscape work and eliminate the current landscaping department. So the company's choices are (a) to continue doing its own work in house or (b) to outsource the work to the contractor. The landscaping department's equipment is generally old, worn out, or obsolete. This is an ideal time for the company to consider whether to replace all the equipment or outsource. Table 14.1 gives Statewide Industries data. Table 14.2 gives the indifference point calculation steps.

If the outsource company were to bid $166,197, the company would break even on the work done. That is, either choice would end up costing the company exactly the same over the 7-year period.

Any outsource contractor's bid above this indifference amount is too high and should not be accepted. If an outsource contractor's bid is below this indifference amount, then outsourcing will reduce the organization's total costs. With an indifference point of $166,197, if the outsource

Table 14.1. Statewide Industries Data

Equipment acquisition cost	$84,000
Straight-line depreciation	
7-year life	
Replacement equipment has no residual value	
Annual depreciation ($84,000 ÷ 7 years)	$12,000
Annual operating costs (labor, equipment repair, etc.)	$140,000
Contractor's bid to perform all landscape work (annual cost)	$175,000
Currently used equipment has no residual value	
Combined Federal and state income tax rate	38%
Cost of capital	16%

Table 14.2. Indifference Point Calculation Steps

Equipment acquisition cost	$84,000
Divided by present value of a 7-year annuity at 16%	÷ 4.038
Equals annual operating cash flow at indifference point	$20,802
Subtract annual depreciation	− $12,000
Equals net income effect at indifference	$8,802
Divided by (1 − tax rate as a decimal; 1 − .38)	÷ 0.62
Equals pretax savings to do work in house at indifference	= $14,197
Add annual in-house costs ($140,000 + $12,000 depreciation)	+ $152,000
Equals indifference point	= $166,197

contractor were to bid to do the work for $164,000 annually, Statewide Industries would save $2,197 ($166,197 − $164,000) annually by accepting the offer and eliminating the in-house department.

There are at least two additional complicating factors that, while realistic, are beyond the intended scope of this book. Most profitable companies would use Modified Accelerated Cost Recovery System depreciation instead of straight-line depreciation. This change in depreciation method would generally favor the in-house choice and require a lower outsource bid to be indifferent.[1] Because the topic of depreciation is a complex one, the reader is encouraged to consult with a tax professional.

We have also disregarded the effect of inflation on either the in-house operating costs or the outsource contractor's price over the multiple-year period being evaluated.[2]

Breakeven and the Cost of Capital

The economic view of the firm leads managers to earn something more than accounting profit in order to generate a return to the owners large enough to offset what the owners could have earned by engaging in some other similar-risk investment. This additional amount of profit is usually discussed in terms of the opportunity cost of capital.

The time value of money theory teaches us that the true breakeven point that considers the opportunity cost plus all other costs will always raise the true total cost, which, in turn, will always raise the breakeven point.

To see an example of factoring in opportunity cost, consider a manufacturing enterprise that makes and sells do-it-yourself home painting equipment. To show the impact of the opportunity cost on the breakeven point, we will first calculate the breakeven point using the traditional approach and then follow up by incorporating the cost of capital into the calculation using a method presented by Brealey, Myers, and Marcus.[3]

Example 2

PowerRoll's most popular product, which represents over 95% of its sales, is its power paint roller on a long handle that pumps paint out of a bucket, up the long handle, and into the roller, helping the painter be more efficient. Their paint roller sells for $25 to hardware stores. Unit variable costs total $12. During one relevant time period the firm sold 21,000 paint rollers through a regional network of neighborhood hardware stores. This earned gross revenues of $525,000. If the firm's fixed costs equal $310,000, the breakeven point is calculated as follows:

$$BE_U = FC \div CM_U$$

$$BE_U = \$310,000 \div (\$25 - \$12) = \$310,000 \div \$13 = 23,846 \text{ Units.}$$

The sale of 21,000 units is below the breakeven point.

Managers at PowerRoll are considering the possibility of purchasing a new $100,000 piece of equipment that has the potential of lowering the unit variable cost from $12 to $10. For now we can assume that the company should be able to sell at least as many rollers in each of the coming years as they have recently. But adding the new equipment will increase the fixed costs by $20,000, bringing total fixed costs up to $330,000. Half of this increase in fixed costs will be depreciation. By using the new equipment, managers expect unit variable costs to decrease. The new breakeven point can be calculated as follows:

$$BE_U = FC \div CM_U$$

$$BE_U = \$330,000 \div (\$25 - \$10) = \$330,000 \div \$15 = 22,000 \text{ Units.}$$

The fixed costs will increase, but managers also expect the unit contribution margin to increase. The net effect is that managers at PowerRoll will find it a little easier to achieve breakeven even though the fixed costs have increased. This illustrates how powerful changes in variable costs can be to lower the breakeven point even under conditions where the fixed costs are increasing.

Spreading the depreciation of the new equipment over 10 years using the straight-line method, the depreciation expense of the new equipment will be $10,000 per year. After the capital investment, annual depreciation will be $10,000.

Table 14.3, PowerRoll Data, is a summary of the business model elements we have established thus far *after* taking into consideration the capital investment and total annual depreciation expense.

We can rewrite this data into an algebra format that puts us on the road to solving for the number of units (q) needed to be sold per year to break even. These data are shown in Table 14.4, Algebraic Format of PowerRoll Data.

To calculate net cash flow, we add the $10,000 in depreciation expense:

$$\text{Annual Cash Flow} = 9.9q - \$207,800.$$

Table 14.3. PowerRoll Data

Capital investment	$100,000
Unit sale price	$25
Unit variable cost	$10
Depreciation	$10,000
Other fixed costs	$320,000
Total fixed costs	$330,000

Table 14.4. *Algebraic Format of PowerRoll Data*

Total sales revenue	$25q
Total variable costs	$10q
Depreciation	$10,000
Total fixed costs	$330,000
Pretax profit	15q – $330,000
Taxes at 34%	5.1q – $112,200
Net profit	9.9q – $217,800

To find the present value of net cash flow, we multiply net cash flow by an annuity factor. The annuity factor operates like net present value in that it helps determine the annual amount of opportunity cost of capital on an investment spanning 10 years at 7% discount rate. To determine the annuity factor, we consult an annuity table for the interest rate per year and the number of years for which the investment is being analyzed (see Appendix E). Alternatively, we can use an annuity formula, which can be found in most business finance books or on the Internet. The appropriate annuity factor for this example is 7.024.

Applying the annuity factor we get the following:

$$\text{Annual Cash Flow Discounted by 7\% Over 10 Years} =$$
$$7.024 \ (9.9q - \$207,800).$$

Now we must account for the $100,000 investment, which is negative cash flow, by placing it in the formula as follows to obtain net cash flow:

$$\text{Net Cash Flow} = -\$100,000 + 7.024 \ (9.9q - \$207,800).$$

Setting the equation to zero and solving for q, we obtain the number of units to break even:

$$0 = -\$100,000 + 7.024 \ (9.9q - \$207,800)$$

$$0 = -\$100,000 + 69.5376q - \$1,459,587.20$$

$$0 = 69.5376q - \$1,559,587.20$$

$$69.5376q = \$1,559,587.20$$

$$q = \$1,559,587.20 \div 69.5376 = 22,428$$
(Rounded Up to Next Whole Unit).

The 7% discount rate is an estimate of the risk the firm faces as it attempts to use its resources to generate future cash flow over time through its business operations. We can estimate the firm's risk by using an approach such as the capital asset pricing model (CAPM), the weighted average cost of capital (WACC), the degree of operating leverage, or a more conservative approach using the risk-free rate of return[4] such as what might be earned from investing in Treasury bills. These are methods described in finance books, which we won't take the time to review here. The 10-year time period is a somewhat arbitrary number of years that managers expect to generate a return over the life of the equipment purchased and used.

The traditional accounting method to calculate breakeven determines that PowerRoll needs to sell 22,000 units. The breakeven method we are exploring here indicates that 22,428 units need to be sold to cover all costs including the cost of capital. Compare these two breakeven amounts in Table 14.5, Comparison of Breakeven Methods.

Table 14.6, Net Income at Economic Breakeven, shows the net income result of selling 22,428 units.

We can call the breakeven point the *economic* breakeven since it attempts to incorporate the opportunity costs of capital into the calculation.

Table 14.5. Comparison of Breakeven Methods

Breakeven using traditional method	Breakeven factoring in opportunity cost	Difference	Difference
22,000 units	22,428 units	428 units	1.9%

Table 14.6. Net Income at Economic Breakeven

Gross sales (22,428 power paint rollers)	$560,700
Less total variable costs at $10 each	$224,280
Contribution margin	$336,420
Less fixed costs	$330,000
Net income before taxes	$6,420

Observations

One observation we can make is that as risk increases and everything else remains unchanged, the economic breakeven point also will increase and as this increases the difference between the accounting method and the economic method is greater.

Economic breakeven method generates a result that is higher than the traditional accounting breakeven method, assuming that the length of the depreciation period is equal to the length of the investment period. As fixed costs increase or as the annuity factor increases, the difference between the two methods of calculation will decrease but will never be precisely equal.

As in other examples we have given in this book, the economic breakeven point must be considered in the context of actual operating conditions. Company operations managers must ask themselves whether the enterprise has the operational capacity to produce the number of units required to achieve economic breakeven. For example, what adjustments might be necessary in terms of scheduling personnel and materials, machine use, maintenance, and outbound logistics? Does sufficient operational slack exist that allows the firm to ramp up production? In some companies, increasing the production may not be possible given the current configuration of assets.

The sales team also must make some judgments regarding the level of demand that can reasonably be stimulated by their efforts in order to achieve economic breakeven. To stimulate this level of demand, will price concessions need to be entertained or will geographic expansion of sales efforts be required and at what additional cost? Estimates of additional costs that might be incurred to produce and sell the economic breakeven amount should be factored into the breakeven calculation.

Variations to the Method

A variation on this, which yields an estimate that is identical to that obtained in the previous analysis, is to take the annual net cash flow and compare it with the amount needed to pay for the annual cost equivalent of the investment when discounted by an annuity factor.[5] This approach treats the payback to the investment as if the company had to earn enough cash to pay an annuity to the shareholders each year. The annual "payment" is the annual opportunity cost of the capital investment. Using a discount rate of 10% and a 10-year life of the investment, we can use the annuity factor of 6.145 (from the annuity formula or an annuity table) in the following equation:

$$\text{Annual Opportunity Cost of Investment} =$$
$$\$1,000,000 \div 10\text{-Year Annuity Factor}$$

$$\text{Annual Opportunity Cost of Investment} =$$
$$\$1,000,000 \div 6.145 = \$162,745.$$

This means that over a 10-year period, in addition to covering all other annual costs, the company must generate annually $162,745 in cash to cover the cost of capital. This means that when the annual net cash flow from the sale of products and the annual opportunity cost are equal, the firm has broken even. Table 14.7, Sensitivity Analysis, illustrates that the firm breaks even when it makes and sells 5,461 units.

The difference between the accounting approach to break even and the interests of economics has been a subject of consideration for decades.[6] In addition to the methods reviewed here, there are other more complex approaches that factor in the cost of capital.[7] You might be interested in reviewing these sometime.

Weaknesses

The economic breakeven method may be considered superior to other methods since it incorporates the time value of money over a period of years. But this method is not perfect. This method implies that variable costs and unit selling prices remain the same over time. One way to overcome this weakness is to adjust the unit variable costs and unit selling price by a reasonable factor such as inflation or other known benchmark. In real life it is unlikely that unit selling prices and unit variable costs will remain stable over several years. They may, in fact, change at different rates.

Future cash flow may be difficult for some small companies to estimate. Using depreciation as the only way to estimate cash flow implies that no other cash flow influences are at work in the business. In reality,

Table 14.7. *Sensitivity Analysis*

DISCOUNT RATE (R)	0.10				
Unit selling price	$2,500	$2,500	$2,500	$2,500	$2,500
Unit variable cost	$1,750	$1,750	$1,750	$1,750	$1,750
Unit contribution margin	$750	$750	$750	$750	$750
Units sold	1,000	3,000	5,461	6,000	8,000
Total revenue	$2,500,000	$7,500,000	$13,652,500	$15,000,000	$20,000,000
Total variable cost	$1,750,000	$5,250,000	$9,556,750	$10,500,000	$14,000,000
Fixed costs (FC)	$4,000,000	$4,000,000	$4,000,000	$4,000,000	$4,000,000
Depreciation (included in FC)	$100,000	$100,000	$100,000	$100,000	$100,000
Pretax profit	($3,250,000)	($1,750,000)	$95,750	$500,000	$2,000,000
Tax at 34%	($1,105,000)	($595,000)	$32,555	$170,000	$680,000
Net profit	($2,145,000)	($1,155,000)	$63,195	$330,000	$1,320,000
Annual net cash flow	($2,045,000)	($1,055,000)	$163,195	$430,000	$1,420,000
Annual opportunity cost on $1M over 10 years at 10%	$162,745	$162,745	$162,745	162,745	$162,745
Difference (net cash flow – annual opportunity cost)	($2,207,745)	($1,217,745)	$450	$267,255	$1,257,255

accounts receivable and accounts payable also influence cash flow, but these are not taken into consideration with the method discussed previously. The wise manager will track down all the various elements that drive cash flow in his or her particular business.

Annual cash flow 5 years from now may be generated from entirely different conditions than currently exist. The capital structure of the organization will likely be different 5 years from now. The NPV method implies that managers will not make adjustments to the business model as the organization proceeds into the future. Even with its weaknesses, one can argue that the traditional accounting method to calculate breakeven ignores the future even more than does the economic method!

Discounted future cash flows are sensitive to the discount rate, which may be difficult to identify for specific projects or particular businesses. Private companies may find it difficult to locate information on comparable companies and the discount rate that should apply.

Ethical Considerations

For the manager whose task is to calculate and report the breakeven point, several ethical considerations should be addressed.[8] For example, managers may attempt to unethically manipulate the outcome of the breakeven calculation in order to achieve some purpose other than finding the truth about breakeven, such as when trying to persuade top-level leaders to increase a capital investment. Ignoring the relevant range or treating some fixed costs as variable costs can manipulate the calculation. Distorting breakeven graphs so that an incorrect conclusion is drawn by the graph user is another way to manipulate the information unethically.

Studying the impact of economic needs of the firm brings into sharp relief one of the fundamental tensions that managers experience. Understanding the breakeven point and the elements of the business model that contribute to breakeven helps a manager appreciate much more deeply the impact of day-to-day operational decisions on the firm's ability to generate wealth. Thus, on one hand, managers want to make economically sound decisions that are responsible to the shareholders. On the other hand, these managers want to make decisions that take into consideration fundamental duties owed to the greater good of society, as well as the decision's impact on the greater good of society.

Ethical values go hand in hand with business values. For example, recognizing the potential harm that can come to a firm's reputation or to one's career when the firm takes advantage of others in order to earn an economic profit, the majority of managers are careful to obey the law and go beyond the letter of the law to do good at the same time as they are doing well economically.

Dynamic markets and regulations constrain managers, making it difficult to achieve an economic profit. Under such constraints managers may be tempted to cut corners, use deceit, or commit fraud to make up for their inability to overcome these barriers.

In most instances, managerial decisions that result in achieving economic breakeven are not in conflict with ethical values. But we should recognize ethical values that managers prize can and do act as constraints on managerial decision making. Not just anything goes[9] if we expect the market economy to continue working efficiently and our brands to maintain strong consumer support. Managers must take into consideration not only the economic goals of the firm but also the greater good of society.

Cognizant of the importance of building shareholder wealth, some managers will choose not to squeeze every nickel and dime out of a company's business model to cover the true total costs when doing so means that they must compromise their ethical values or in other ways bring harm to the greater good of society. Taking the perspective that life does not consist solely in the abundance of possessions such as wealth-building assets, under some circumstances managers may be willing to forgo a portion of the economic profit for the sake of employees, other stakeholders such as customers, or the environment shared in common by society.

CHAPTER 15

Quadratic Equation

It can be argued that when the relevant range is used, the traditional breakeven formula shows a relatively linear relationship between quantity and cost and revenue. The basic formula for breakeven analysis also assumes that the business situation is unchanging in terms of selling price, unit variable costs, fixed costs, product mix, and a host of other variables that can affect both revenue and costs. Can we calculate breakeven when either the revenue curve or the cost curve is changing? For example, a company may face new competitors in the market that offer more choices for customers. These companies enter the market for the product because the investors believe they can capture cash value from customers if demand is on the increase. More companies entering the market tends to increase customer responsiveness to price changes (price elasticity of demand).

As customer responsiveness increases, it becomes increasingly difficult to win new customers and keep current customers. The entrance of new competitors in the market usually results in incumbents reacting to this by lowering their prices. Lowering prices makes the revenue curve change as more units are produced and sold. Total revenue begins to decline as more and more units are sold. The cost curve may continue to be a linear relationship: Our variable costs are unchanged, and our fixed costs are the same.

If the revenue curve drops low enough (because we continue to lower prices), we could very well anticipate a time when we drop the price too low and sell units at a loss. If this occurs, we should expect to find two breakeven points, not just one. In practical terms, we will need to be as concerned about selling too many products if our prices get too low as we would be in attempting to sell enough products to break even.

Changes in Revenue

Consider the following simple example of historical data from a company that makes an unusual type of MP3 player.[1] See Table 15.1, Revenue and Costs. As more units are produced, competitors jump into the market and the market price declines.

Using a statistics software application or a spreadsheet application that contains statistical functions, we can determine the formulas for both the total revenue curve and the total cost curve. We can also graph this table using spreadsheet software.

For this example, the formulas for the two curves are as follows:

$$R(x) = (-x^2 \div 1000) + 10x$$

Table 15.1. Revenue and Costs

x	$R(x)$	$C(x)$
0	0	7,000
500	4,750	8,000
1,000	9,000	9,000
1,500	12,750	10,000
2,000	16,000	11,000
2,500	18,750	12,000
3,000	21,000	13,000
3,500	22,750	14,000
4,000	24,000	15,000
4,500	24,750	16,000
5,000	25,000	17,000
5,500	24,750	18,000
6,000	24,000	19,000
6,500	22,750	20,000
7,000	21,000	21,000
7,500	18,750	22,000

Where

x	=	Number of MP3 Players Produced and Sold
$R(x)$	=	Total Revenue
$C(x)$	=	Total Cost

$$C(x) = 7000 + 2x.$$

You may recall from high school algebra that the form the formula for $R(x)$ takes is called a polynomial.

We know the breakeven point is the point where total revenue equals total cost, or

$$R(x) = C(x).$$

So we can substitute the two curve formulas in this equation as follows and solve for x since x is the number of units of our MP3 player that we are concerned about:

$$R(x) = C(x)$$

$$(-x^2 \div 1000) + 10x = 7000 + 2x.$$

If we set this polynomial formula equal to zero, we get the following:

$$(-x^2 \div 1000) + 8x - 7000 = 0.$$

You may remember from high school math class that the polynomial equation is known as the quadratic equation: $ax^2 + bx + c$. To solve for x in a quadratic equation, we can use the famous quadratic formula:

$$x = \frac{-b \pm \sqrt{b^2 - 4ac}}{2a}$$

In so doing, we come up with the following results:

$$x = 8,000 \pm 6,000 \div 2$$

$$x = 1,000, x = 7,000.$$

As the graph (plotted using spreadsheet software) in Figure 15.1, Multiple Breakeven Points—Linear Cost Curve, shows, our two breakeven points are at 1,000 units and 7,000 units.

In practice, company decision makers will watch the impact of falling prices on the cost-volume-profit relationship. This graph shows that if the decision makers don't do anything different except drop the price, they will reach the upper breakeven point at 7,000 units. If the market price continues to drop, the company must either find a way to differentiate its product from that of competitors so it can keep its prices higher than what other

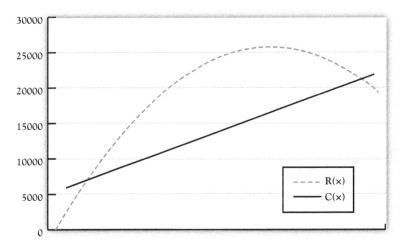

Figure 15.1. Multiple Breakeven Points—Linear Cost Curve

companies charge, or it must find ways to decrease its fixed costs, unit costs, or both. This illustrates why companies in highly competitive markets where the price elasticity of demand is changing (in an unfavorable direction, i.e., increasing) and where opportunities to differentiate one company from another exert more effort to find ways to lower their costs. To maintain profitability, they are being chased by the upper breakeven point!

Costs and Revenue Changing

Depending on the specific situation, a company may also face the unsavory scenario in which both costs and revenue are changing in unfavorable directions. By extending Barnett and Ziegler's[2] approach, we now have total revenue curve and the total cost curve nonlinear (changing) as illustrated in Figure 15.2, Nonlinear Cost and Revenue Curves.

This graph visually indicates that something unpleasant is happening to the company's ability to grow its total revenue. In addition, unit variable costs are increasing rather than staying static. It could be that the supply of an important ingredient used in the product is decreasing, thus driving the cost of that ingredient ever higher. There could be other factors that bring relatively rapid changes to the cost of production and distribution such as energy costs. Consider Table 15.2, Changing Revenue and Costs, which was used to generate the graph.

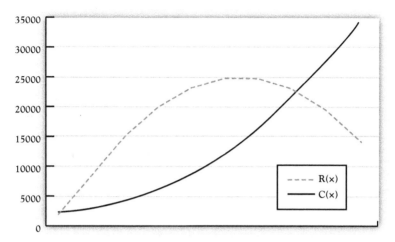

Figure 15.2. Nonlinear Cost and Revenue Curves

Table 15.2. Changing Revenue and Costs

x	C(x)	R(x)
100	20,225	17,180
500	24,125	79,500
1,000	35,750	143,000
1,500	54,875	190,500
2,000	81,500	222,000
2,500	115,625	237,500
3,000	157,250	237,000
3,500	206,375	220,500
4,000	263,000	188,000

The following are the formulas for the two curves on the graph:

$$R(x) = -0.032\,x^2 + 175x$$

$$C(x) = 0.015x^2 + 0.75x + 20,000.$$

As in the previous example, $R(x) = C(x)$ at the breakeven point(s). We can follow the same procedure using the quadratic equation and the quadratic formula as follows:

$$-0.032\,x^2 + 175x = 0.015x^2 + 0.75x + 20,000$$

$$-.047x^2 + 174.25x - 20,000 = 0.$$

Using the quadratic formula to solve for x, we get the following:

$$x = (-174.25 + 161.104) / -0.094 = 140 \text{ Units (After Rounding)}$$

$$x = (-174.25 - 161.104) / -0.094 = 3,568 \text{ Units.}$$

Notice that if unit variable costs had remained unchanged, the upper breakeven point would be higher than it is when unit variable costs increase. On the following graph shown in Figure 15.3, Comparison of Breakeven Points, the dotted line represents unit variable costs that are linear (unchanging). Notice what happens to the breakeven point! It moves to the right.

In other words, as unit variable costs *increase*, the upper breakeven point decreases over what it might have been if unit variable costs had remained unchanged. If the company can work diligently to keep its unit variable costs stable (such as signing a long-term contract for a key factor used in production or distribution), it can weather the storm of decreasing market prices longer than its competitors can.

Interestingly, once we know the formula for the total cost curve and the total revenue curve, we can also calculate the production/sales level where profit is at its maximum.

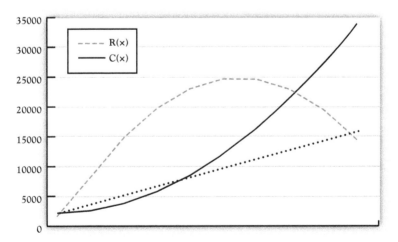

Figure 15.3. Comparison of Breakeven Points

Limitations

We know that the basic breakeven formula has serious limitations imposed by the fairly severe assumptions required. Using polynomial equations to estimate breakeven carries its own limitations. First, a polynomial curve such as for total revenue assumes that total revenue will cross the zero line at least twice. Of course, revenue is zero before any units are sold. But at the upper end of the curve, crossing zero usually will occur only when the firm stops selling products. In other words, the polynomial equation may not hold true at the upper end of the curve if the company decision makers respond to their environment by cranking up advertising to stimulate demand, coming out with different products that reinvigorate the revenue curve. Likewise, the polynomial total cost curve assumes that total costs will continue to rise infinitely. While it feels like this is happening in volatile markets, company decision makers normally will make adjustments to keep infinite costs from being incurred.

A second weakness of this approach may also be a strength. This approach to estimating breakeven does not identify which unit variable costs are the culprits for driving up the total cost curve. It just alerts decision makers that unit variable costs are changing rather than static. This, however, is the method's strength; since all costs and the net changes of these costs are rolled into the total cost curve, we don't have to know which specific unit variable costs are contributing to the changes just to find out that the net changes are moving us away from a linear relationship. Of course, it can be argued that wise decision makers who are monitoring the business situation will be aware of some of these. For example, when the price of crude oil rises by 10% for 10 successive months, this in itself tends to get decision makers' attention.

Third, we must say that it is the net effect of changes in total costs. Some costs will change unfavorably (increase), but other costs may decrease. When unit variable costs are changing in an unfavorable direction, we expect managers to adapt by cutting costs elsewhere in the organization where possible, finding alternate suppliers, negotiating better terms on agreements, or making other adjustments to mitigate the effect of the changes. Thus, just like the basic breakeven formula that portrays a business situation at a point in time, so does the polynomial, quadratic equation approach, the difference being that the quadratic equation method shows a point in time that is changing.

A fourth concern is that this method depends on historical data or on accurate projections of changes that are expected to take place in the future. Breakeven has traditionally depended on historical data even when making informed projections into the future. Historical data[3] do not show what might have occurred if managers had exercised closer controls. Neither do they anticipate accurately what managers will do in the future to prevent unfriendly changes to the breakeven point. Historical data are time, place, and context dependent. What may have been appropriate last year in terms of changing (or not) costs and revenue may not be the conditions today or tomorrow. Just like its linear counterpart, the quadratic equation approach must be used in conjunction with wise managerial decisions to improve control over costs or to improve the firm's ability to continue capturing revenue from customers who may have more substitute choices tomorrow than they do today.

As you may have noted, this approach is rooted in the economics of a given situation. A fifth weakness is that only the impact of substitutes (on price elasticity of demand) may be under consideration when complements also have an effect on price elasticity of demand. Changes in total revenue may occur simply because a competitor has found a way to drastically cut its total cost curve using new technology (either hardware or work processes). Changes in complementary products (products that are used with your firm's product or are in some way necessary for the customer to gain optimum value when buying your firm's product) can affect the total revenue curve.[4] The approach using quadratic equations is silent regarding this.

A sixth limitation is that since all factors that affect costs and revenue are "thrown in" (some would say "with the kitchen sink"), this approach is too broad to be of use in making specific decisions.

A seventh limitation is that the amount of historical data needed to accurately estimate the formula for the cost curve or revenue curve may be greater than decision makers can offer. Generally, we would like to see a minimum of 30 to 50 data points to apply statistical analysis. This raises the issue of the limits on the statistical precision by estimating the cost curve and revenue curve formulas. Data from real life usually do not line up in a clean, smooth curve. Thus, estimating the "best fit" of the curve always comes with a degree of error. Such error can lead the decision maker to underestimate or overestimate the breakeven point. It must be remembered, however, that performing any kind of breakeven analysis (linear or otherwise) is always an estimate.

CHAPTER 16

Tax Effects on Cost-Volume-Profit

Throughout this book, we have disregarded the effect of income taxes on cost-volume-profit analysis. When an organization is at breakeven, this disregard of income taxes is appropriate because the organization is earning no profit and suffering no loss, and therefore incurring no income tax liability. Furthermore, even when an organization is earning a profit, many users of cost-volume-profit analysis are not responsible for the company's tax issues, tax decisions, and tax effects. They just need to show how a product, department, or idea can be profitable to the firm.

However, when the organization moves away from the breakeven point and begins to earn a profit, some level of management must realistically include income taxes in their calculations.

Returning to the target profit applications of chapter 4, we can modify the target profit formulas to incorporate the effect of income taxes. Here is the formula:[1]

$$\frac{\text{Fixed Costs} + \left(\dfrac{\text{Desired After-Tax Profit}}{1 - \text{Income Tax Rate}} \right)}{\text{Contribution Margin per Unit}} = \begin{array}{l} \text{Units to Be Sold to} \\ \text{Reach Desired Profit.} \end{array}$$

Assume management has set its annual desired after-tax profit at $52,000. Using the data from the first example in chapter 4, let's calculate the number of units that must be sold to reach the target.

Annual Fixed Costs = $520,000

Selling Price per Unit = $25

Variable Cost per Unit = $17

$$\text{Contribution Margin (CM) per Unit} = \$8$$

$$\text{Annual Desired After-Tax Profit} = \$52,000$$

$$\text{Income Tax Rate} = 35\%$$

$$\cfrac{\$520,000 \text{ Annual Fixed Costs} + \left(\cfrac{\$52,000 \text{ Desired After-Tax Profit}}{0.65} \right)}{\$8 \text{ CM per Unit}} = \begin{array}{l} 75,000 \text{ Units to} \\ \text{Be Sold Annually} \end{array}$$

As with the basic breakeven calculation, we can calculate the sales dollars required to reach the desired profit.

$$\cfrac{\$520,000 \text{ Annual Fixed Costs} + \left(\cfrac{\$52,000 \text{ Desired After-Tax Profit}}{0.65} \right)}{0.32 \text{ CM Ratio}} = \begin{array}{l} \$1,875,000 \\ \text{Annual Sales} \end{array}$$

Alternatively, management might express its profit objective as an amount per unit of sales, a variable target profit. The formula to include the income tax effect would be modified this way:

$$\cfrac{\text{Fixed Costs}}{\text{Contribution Margin per Unit} - \left(\cfrac{\text{Desired After-Tax Profit per Unit}}{1 - \text{Income Tax Rate}} \right)} = \begin{array}{l} \text{Units Sold to} \\ \text{Achieve Desired} \\ \text{Profit.} \end{array}$$

Here are our data:

$$\text{Annual Fixed Costs} = \$520,000$$

$$\text{Selling Price per Unit} = \$25$$

$$\text{Variable Cost per Unit} = \$17$$

$$\text{Contribution Margin per Unit} = \$8$$

$$\text{Desired After-Tax Profit per Unit} = \$1.95$$

Income Tax Rate = 35%

$$\frac{\$520,000 \text{ Annual Fixed Costs}}{\$8 \text{ CM Per Unit} - \left(\dfrac{\begin{array}{c}\$1.95 \text{ Desired} \\ \text{After-Tax Profit}\end{array}}{0.65} \right)} = \begin{array}{l}104,000 \\ \text{Units to} \\ \text{Be Sold} \\ \text{Annually}\end{array}$$

Again, the sales dollars required to achieve the target profit can be calculated. We will have to calculate the after-tax contribution margin and contribution margin ratio:

$$\$8 \text{ CM Per Unit} - (\$1.95 \text{ After-Tax Profit per Unit} \div 0.65) =$$
$$\$8 - \$3 = \$5 \text{ After-Tax CM per Unit.}$$

Then, the CM ratio is $\$5 \div \$25 = 0.20$. Now calculate the annual sales dollars needed.

$$\frac{\$520,000 \text{ Annual Fixed Costs}}{0.20 \text{ After-Tax CM Ratio}} = \begin{array}{l}\$2,600,000 \\ \text{Annual Sales}\end{array}$$

APPENDIX A

Glossary

To establish a common set of terms that we use in this book, we offer the following.

Breakeven

Breakeven has traditionally been defined in at least five different ways. The five ways use different data to bring you to break even.

1. Net income equals zero.
2. Total revenue equals total costs.
3. Total revenue equals total variable costs plus total fixed costs.
4. Total contribution margin equals total fixed costs.
5. Net present value equals zero.

Business Model

A business model is your plan for your business, briefly expressed in simple terms and simple structure. It may be written in outline form or as bullet points. The concepts and calculations of breakeven and cost-volume-profit analysis (explained later), as part of your business model, show you how much work you must do to pay your costs and achieve profitability.

The business model is composed of two elements: (a) a story that describes how the enterprise works and the key assumptions that support the story and (b) financial estimates that describe the way the organization will add profit for investors as a result of the operations of the revenue stream and expense structure.[1] The revenue stream and expense structure are built on assumptions (the story) about how the organization operates in its environment. The business model can be expressed in terms of any one of several typical financial statements and analyses such as the following: the income statement, the statement of cash flows, the balance sheet, and breakeven (cost-volume-profit) analysis.

When developing the assumptions regarding the revenue stream, several questions are used, such as the following: Who are the target customers and what do they value? What do we assume regarding demand, price elasticity of demand, and the likely actions of competitors to woo away our customers? How do we make money from delivering value to our customers? How do the marketing and distribution channel relationships work *downstream* from the firm? How do the collaboration arrangements work with other organizations that direct customers toward the firm or that complement us by delivering additional value to customers?

Likewise, the expense structure is based on many assumptions, such as these: How do the distribution channel and other collaboration relationships work *upstream* from the firm (e.g., suppliers)? What is the price elasticity of supply? What bargaining power does the firm have with various suppliers? What is the structure of costs from core capabilities required to deliver value to customers on a consistent basis? What are the fixed and variable costs incurred from delivering value to customers? As the complexity of the business increases, the number and complexity of the assumptions also increases. See Figure A.1, The Business Model.

The value of the business model as a projection or decision-making device is dependent entirely on the accuracy of the assumptions that are used. Entrepreneurs and other managers develop increasingly realistic

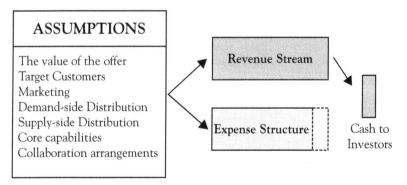

Figure A.1. The Business Model

assumptions as they gain experience. Potential investors evaluate the accuracy of the assumptions when determining whether to invest in the firm. However, judgments regarding assumptions are subject to the same biases and errors as are other managerial judgments.[2] For example, unwarranted optimism is a problem for all managers. This can lead the manager to accept overly optimistic assumptions regarding the revenue stream as well as being overly optimistic regarding the ability of the firm to keep costs low.

Contribution Margin

Total revenue minus total variable costs equals total contribution margin. Contribution margin per unit is calculated revenue (selling price) per unit minus variable cost per unit.

Certain types of organizations tend to exhibit certain cost behaviors. For example, universities, hospitals, and accounting and law firms tend to have a high proportion of their costs as fixed costs and a relatively small proportion of their costs as variable costs. This means that those organizations tend to have (and need) very high contribution margins per unit of sales.

Contribution Margin Ratio

Contribution margin per unit divided by unit selling price is the contribution margin ratio. Alternatively, total contribution margin divided by total revenue is the contribution margin ratio. These calculations will produce identical results. The result is usually interpreted as a percentage. For example, if the contribution margin per unit is $7 and the selling price per unit is $10, the contribution margin ratio is 70%.

Cost of Goods Sold

The cost of goods sold is the full cost to purchase or produce the goods your business offers for sale to customers.

Cost-Volume-Profit Analysis

Cost-volume-profit analysis is the application of the breakeven concept. It may include calculation of a breakeven point, modification to allow for profit, and visual presentation of the results on a graph.

Successfully applying the concepts and methods of cost-volume-profit analysis requires that fixed and variable costs be accurately identified and measured. Traditional accounting and financial reporting systems, designed to comply with generally accepted accounting principles, do not provide the fixed and variable cost and contribution margin information necessary for cost-volume-profit analysis.

Fixed Costs

Fixed costs may be viewed in two ways:

1. Fixed costs *per unit* change in inverse proportion as the quantity (volume) of units sold increases or decreases.
2. Fixed costs *in total* do not change as the quantity (volume) of units sold increases or decreases. Total fixed costs *can* change. Inflation may increase fixed costs and deflation may decrease fixed costs while the quantity of units sold remains constant. Additionally, management decisions to change technology or capacity generally change total fixed costs incurred.

Here is an illustration of fixed cost behavior. City Transit Authority calculates the fuel cost of one bus for one day at $150. If 100 people ride that bus during a day, the fuel cost is $1.50 per rider ($150 ÷ 100 people). If 250 people ride the bus during a day, the fuel cost per rider drops to $.60 ($150 ÷ 250 people).

High-Low Method

The high-low method is a simple method to separate a mixed cost into its variable and fixed cost components. This method considers only the highest cost and the lowest cost incurred during the time period and disregards all other cost information.

Least Squares Method

The least squares method (also called the linear regression method) is a mathematical approach to separate a mixed cost into its variable and fixed cost components. This method, in contrast to the high-low method, considers all available data of costs incurred during the time period. Viewed as a formula, this method may seem intimidating and difficult to use. In this book, we explain how to easily apply the linear regression method using Excel spreadsheet commands.

Mixed Costs

Mixed costs contain some variable costs and some fixed costs, presented as a single amount. A simple example of a mixed cost is the compensation of a salesperson who receives a fixed salary per month plus a commission (a percentage of sales, a variable amount).

If the organization has no history or operating data for a particular cost, an engineering analysis may be conducted to determine the types and amounts of costs.[3]

When there is historical data for a particular cost, there are several methods available to separate a mixed cost into its variable and fixed components. We will consider two of the more commonly used methods next.

Net Present Value

The net present value compares the acquisition or implementation cost of a long-life asset, project, or opportunity against the cash expected to be received from that asset, project, or opportunity over a period of 2 or more future years. All revenue and cost amounts are modified (discounted) using time value of money techniques.

Relevant Range

The relevant range is the capacity a company has to produce and sell goods and/or services without incurring additional fixed costs. A factory operating one 8-hour shift per day may have the capacity to produce 50,000 units per year. If that factory begins operating two 8-hours shifts per day, it has the capacity to produce 100,000 units per year. Many of the factory's operating costs, which are fixed as long as the factory runs only 8 hours per day, will increase (perhaps double) when the factory begins running 16 hours per day.

Sales Mix

The sales mix is the specific product and/or services offered for sale by a business and the relative proportion of sales of each product or service line. An appliance store might have a sales mix of 70% General Electric products and 30% Whirlpool products. Alternatively, that appliance store might have a sales mix of 80% of total revenue coming from appliances sold and 20% of total revenue coming from appliance repair service.

Total Costs

Total costs include all variable costs and all fixed costs of your business. From an accounting perspective, these are the total costs. From an economic perspective, total costs include these costs as well as the more hidden opportunity cost of capital.

Total Revenue

Total revenue is the amount charged all customers for goods and/or services they purchased from your company during the period being measured (typically month, quarter, or year). This amount may alternatively be called total sales.

Traditional Breakeven Formula

Traditionally, breakeven has been expressed in one of two ways. If the desired result is the quantity of units that must be sold to achieve breakeven, the following formula is used:

$$\frac{\text{Fixed Costs}}{\text{Contribution Margin per Unit}} = \text{Breakeven in Units to Be Sold} = BE_U.$$

If the desired result is the dollar amount of sales required to reach breakeven, the following formula is used:

$$\frac{\text{Fixed Costs}}{\begin{array}{c}\text{Contribution Margin}\\ \text{Ratio per Unit}\end{array}} = \text{Breakeven in Dollars to Be Sold} = BE_\$.$$

Unit

A unit is the item being measured. An appliance store could consider one unit of sales when one refrigerator was sold. The expression "unit" may take on different meanings. An airline might consider one unit as one ticket sold to a passenger, or it might consider one unit as one flight from point of departure to point of arrival.

Why does clearly identifying the unit of measure matter? The identification of variable costs, contribution margin, and relevant range all depend on the definition of a "unit."

Unit Selling Price

The unit selling price is the price your business charges a customer per item sold.

Variable Costs

Variable costs may be viewed in two ways:

1. Variable costs *per unit* do not change as the quantity (volume) of units sold increases or decreases.
2. Variable costs *in total* change proportionally as the quantity (volume) of units sold increases or decreases.

Here is an illustration of variable cost behavior. Bill mows lawns during the summer months. He typically spends $1 for fuel for his lawnmower per lawn mowed. During May, with plenty of rain and cool temperatures, the grass grew rapidly and Bill mowed 40 lawns. Consequently, he spent $40 for fuel that month. During July, when the weather was hot and dry, Bill mowed only 20 lawns and spent only $20 for fuel.

The distinction between variable cost and fixed cost can be at least partially a management decision. Labor costs may be variable if workers are paid hourly and the quantity of labor hired is adjusted more or less continuously, based on need. Conversely, labor costs may be fixed if there are union contracts that guarantee both hours paid and the rate of pay or if the number of employees is relatively constant and employees are paid on salary.[4]

Weighted Mean

The mean is the arithmetic average of two or more values. The mean of 7 and 3 is 5. The weighted mean (also referred to as the weighted average) assigns a proportionally greater value to some items or units and a proportionally smaller value to others. Here is a simple retail store example:

4 People Spent $20 Each

2 People Spent $10 Each

Simple Mean of Selling Prices: ($20 + $10) ÷ 2 = $15

Weighted Mean of Sales per Customer: (4 × $20) + (2 × $10) ÷ 6 customers = $16.67 (Rounded)

APPENDIX B

Limitations and Criticisms

The breakeven concept and the techniques of cost-volume-profit analysis are powerful business tools. Understanding them and applying them correctly can be an important part of achieving success in business. However, these tools, powerful as they are, have their limitations. Recognizing these limitations is essential to correctly understanding and using cost-volume-profit analysis.[1] Here are the commonly recognized limitations:

- *Linearity.* The first limitation is that revenues and costs are assumed to be linear. That means the selling price per unit would never change and every customer would pay exactly the same price per unit. It also means that variable costs would be exactly the same for every unit. There is no provision for discounts to be received on materials purchased or fluctuating overtime premium to be paid to employees who work different quantities of extra hours.
- *Relevant range.* The company would always operate within the relevant range. There would never be a need to increase or decrease capacity.
- *Productivity.* Productivity or technological changes would not occur to change the behavior of costs from variable to fixed. Over the history of business, technology and productivity have not been static. The shift from labor-intensive to capital-intensive industry converted some formerly variable costs to fixed costs. The same change in cost behavior (away from variable to fixed) has occurred in retail and service businesses as technology has reduced or replaced human labor with bar code readers and computer software.[2]
- *Inventory.* There would be no change in the amount of inventory carried by the company. The quantity of units sold would

always equal the quantity purchased and/or produced. For manufacturing firms, generally accepted accounting principles divide the costs of production between unsold inventory (on the balance sheet) and sold units (on the income statement). This cost allocation presents no problem for variable costs. However, it is a problem with regard to fixed production costs when the quantity of goods produced is not the same as the quantity sold. Cost-volume-profit analysis requires that all fixed costs be accumulated for use in the analysis.

- *Inflation.* There would be no inflation or deflation. Inflation and deflation tend to make fixed costs appear variable. When performing a cost analysis of utilities (such as water, electricity, and natural gas) or fuel (gasoline, for example), the actual units consumed may be used in lieu of the dollar cost to eliminate the effects of inflation or deflation.

- *Sales mix.* If the company sells more than one product or service, the sales mix would remain constant.

- *Accounting information.* The accounting records are adequate and appropriate to accurately identify and measure variable and fixed costs.

- *Opportunity cost.* The traditional accounting approach to calculating breakeven assumes that the opportunity costs of the business model are zero when multiple years are considered.

Criticisms

Criticisms of breakeven analysis' conceptual weaknesses historically have followed its journey since its inception.

- *Simplicity.* The limitations of using the basic, traditional breakeven formula have been discussed by many.[3] One of the early reviews of criticisms was performed by Joel Dean[4] of Columbia University. He describes four limitations: (a) the difficulty of estimating costs, (b) oversimplifying the revenue function by assuming that price remains constant, (c) considering the forces that influence the company as static rather than dynamic, and (d) the fact that managers adapt to changing conditions. This set of criticisms essentially focuses on the *simplicity* of breakeven analysis used in the presence of complex organizations and their changing environments. Here is a case where the strength of breakeven also carries a weakness. The simplicity of traditional breakeven formulas and the assumptions on which they are based require decision makers to think in terms of single products, simple variables, static relationships, a single and considered relatively static period of time, and costs divided into two categories (fixed or variable). The static nature of breakeven assumptions does not reflect the reality that makes up a dynamic complicated market. Breakeven analysis simply takes a snapshot. Wise managers do not think in terms of single points in time with nothing changing. Rather, they think in terms of what will change given where they have been in the past and the current situation.

• *Isolation.* Another criticism of breakeven analysis focuses on the relative *isolation* that decision makers place themselves in when using breakeven analysis. Financial decisions, marketing decisions, and operational decisions are integrated in real life, but the data needed to make these decisions are often not integrated. Each data set comes from a different place in the organization and represents just one variable. This makes the job of a decision maker difficult. For example, production data on the number of units produced over a given time frame is distinctly different from the economic data estimating market demand or price elasticity of demand. In turn, marketing data are by nature different than the financial information. In real life, changes in production volume affect pricing, which affects price elasticity of demand and also affects the cost of materials used in production. The isolation of marketing from operations from finance is partly a result of organizational specialization. Operational managers typically are focused on creating efficiencies in their operational departments. This specialized focus tends to isolate them from the chief concerns that financial decision makers have or the priorities that marketing decision makers think are important.[5] Although breakeven analysis formula is criticized, it is one tool to help overcome the problem of organizational complexity. The fundamental challenge of coordination never goes away even as we continue to see new generations of technology become available. Breakeven analysis was developed, in part, as one way to improve coordination of effort. When marketing, operations, and finance managers of a company come together to coordinate their efforts, they all are using breakeven thinking and language though perhaps from their own specialist perspective.

One of the difficulties in developing organization-wide systemic thinking[6] is the inability of leaders to overcome parochial barriers ("silos") that separate departments. Breakeven analysis and breakeven thinking when used in cross-departmental discussions is one tool that can break down these barriers.

Managers and scholars alike have come to understand that the last frontier of sustainable competitive advantage lies in the organizational abilities that are difficult to copy.[7] Central to this is consistent coordination of effort across the entire value chain of an organization as it connects with suppliers and customers. Helping managers of all key functional areas of an organization to develop their breakeven thinking abilities and then to use these abilities collectively as they coordinate their efforts with each other offers the possibility that competitive advantages gained from organizational efforts also will be sustained *profitably*. Without the widespread use of breakeven thinking, profitable coordination of effort becomes more difficult. One might even argue that coordination of effort without the wide use of breakeven thinking in the organization can result in the coordination of *unprofitability*. In short, for sustainable competitive advantages truly to remain advantageous, breakeven analysis must become one of the standard, frequently used tools in every department and every level of the organization from front-line workers and first-level supervisors to the directors in the boardrooms.

Criticisms of these tools result in a paradox. On one hand, it is easy to criticize the fairly simple formula for not representing complex, dynamic circumstances. On the other hand, many managers continue to use simple breakeven analysis to help them bring dynamic thinking to the business problems they face. In spite of its many limitations and criticisms, breakeven continues to be one of the best ways to focus on the relationship between cost, volume, and profitability.[8]

APPENDIX C

A Short Genealogy of Breakeven Analysis

One could argue that the thinking behind breakeven analysis has been in use for centuries if not millennia. The development of breakeven formulas and charts, like many ideas in management, appears to have emerged out of the rich history of 19th-century economics. In practice, several streams of thought contributed to the development of the breakeven tools represented in this book: the applicability of cost accounting in managerial decision making and the emphasis on efficiency, a legacy of the turbulent scientific management movement, played a part in bringing breakeven analysis to the forefront. Out of this social context, marginal analysis, the concept of the economic *indifference* point, and then cost-volume-profit analysis emerged.

Business leaders in decades surrounding the transition from the 19th to the 20th century were focused on ways to increase efficiency. Businesses, especially manufacturing and the railroads, were growing in size and, because of division of labor, increasing in complexity. This growth made the process of profit-oriented decision making increasingly difficult.

Products could be shipped rapidly over long distances as at no other time in history. More and more products were heading toward commodity-like price competition, which in turn squeezed profit margins, making it more crucial to get right the profit-volume decisions.

Railroads influenced the development of modern organizations and communication systems. Downward pressure on prices from buyers of transportation services influenced railroad executives to sharpen their abilities to understand the relationships between costs, volume, and profit. As railroads opened up distribution of products into new markets, larger quantities of products became available. Commodities could be shipped from the firms of Kansas and Missouri and reach the metropolitan markets of Chicago, Philadelphia, and New York within hours. A growing middle class with income to spend solidified demand for these manufactured goods. But as the volume of production increased to meet the growing demand, the profitability of these companies changed. The speed of decision making increased to match the increased speed in distribution and communication. Managers needed better tools to understand the impact of changing cost and revenue structures on the ability of the firm to generate a profit. In 1887 railroad engineer A. M. Wellington discussed how high fixed costs placed railroads at risk if they lost business. However, Wellington did not produce a breakeven formula to illustrate his point.

Differences in perspective between a company's engineers and its business managers were starting to be recognized as barriers to further developments in the ability to be profitable.[1] In spite of Frederick Taylor's attempts to bridge the gap between management and labor with a scientific approach to management, the age-old conflicts between the two groups were increasing in their intensity, with both sides becoming more sophisticated in how they understood business.

Management and management engineers needed better tools for decision making and for communication with each other.[2] Managers started using breakeven charts.

One of the earliest focused studies of the topic in the United States came from the work of Henry Hess.[3] In 1904 an article by John Mann appeared in the *Encyclopedia of Accounting* showing the methods for preparing breakeven charts.[4] As principles of cost accounting began to mature in the 1920s, the concepts of fixed costs and variable costs came to have wider applications than in just financial accounting.[5] It was the scientific management movement that brought together these developing streams of thought, which resulted in the creation of the simple breakeven formula we know today. Thus, in 1922 John Williams published an article in the *Bulletin of the Taylor Society* that described the mathematical formula for breakeven.[6]

Organizational problems began to arise from increased size and complexity. A few years later J. O. McKinsey[7] proposed that breakeven charts be used in discussions between sales, production, and finance decision makers. McKinsey's recommendation, largely forgotten today, is that breakeven analysis should be conducted periodically for each operating unit of a company. The reason for this is that operating unit fixed costs and variable costs will vary from unit to unit. They can change with other changes taking place in the business or in the firm's larger environment. Because of this, the sales volume necessary to generate return on invested capital also will vary by unit. At the end of each period, unit managers from sales, operations, and finance would come together to discuss their current situation and what they expected for the near-term future. Such discussions are designed to coordinate divergent areas of emphasis and integrate divergent ways of thinking.

Breakeven analysis provided an important connecting link between the assumptions that managers had about their business, the external environment, and actual business activities. It became and remains one of the more popular managerial accounting tools.

Since its introduction decades ago, the breakeven concept has been enhanced, adjusted, and extended in an attempt to reduce or correct for its limitations and make it applicable to more and more business situations. During the 1940s, 1950s, and 1960s, accounting scholars and practitioners[8] published articles reviewing various facets of breakeven and its use. Periodically after these three decades practicing managers and scholars made additional contributions to the subject. For example, Martin[9] showed how to relate breakeven point from one year to another while taking into consideration the cost of capital, and Creese[10] explored breakeven when the production quantity is fixed but the time period changes. Scholars proposed more precise and sophisticated approaches to breakeven analysis, using statistical tools when conditions are uncertain.[11]

Gardner, Tse, and then a generation later, Schweitzer, Trossmann, and Lawson became the first to offer book-length treatments of the topic.[12] The last of these three emphasized the academic, theoretical dimensions of the concept. For many users of breakeven methods, these three books have been forgotten, though the wisdom they contain is as relevant today as when they were written.

Before and after these books many articles have been published demonstrating specific, practical applications of breakeven analysis or evaluating its limitations as a management decision-making tool. Some scholars experimented with various ways to extend the basic concepts, while others clarified the limitations of breakeven.

Breakeven analysis has become a traditional component of introductory accounting, marketing, management, and entrepreneurship textbooks. A common feature of these texts is that, probably due to space limitations, such books typically present just one or two of the most basic methods to teach the concept. More advanced managerial accounting, managerial economics, and business finance texts also include short sections on breakeven. By the time undergraduate students arrive at their senior capstone course, they are expected to understand breakeven analysis when analyzing cases. Sadly, the few applications found in introductory textbooks do not adequately prepare students to determine whether the firms they study are breaking even.

What has been lacking for several years is a product that collects and explores the practical applications of breakeven thinking useful to a variety of industries and decision situations, but that is not so academic as to put off many busy practicing managers. We present in this book the applications and approaches we believe most managers will find useful, leaving the more complicated methods to explore another day. Thus, this book is not intended to be a comprehensive encyclopedia of breakeven methods but rather a practical analytic tool belt that practicing managers and students can relatively quickly add to their business decision-making skills.

The activity of calculating the breakeven point is necessary for just about every organization in existence. It is difficult to think of even one example where the entrepreneurs and the venture capitalists or angel investors of start-up companies would not be interested in knowing the breakeven point for their venture. Likewise, corporate entrepreneurs starting new profit centers use breakeven thinking. Years ago, when manufacturing firms were focusing on making a profit producing and selling one or two products, the basic formula worked well. But life has changed. Service businesses now dominate the market landscape. Now breakeven analysis is employed to help decision makers solve problems that encompass the context of the entire value chain of the firm at the same time as solving specific operational problems.

APPENDIX D

Using Breakeven Thinking to Decide Whether to Start a Business

Breakeven thinking begins before you start a business. For example, starting your own golf course and pro-shop business requires that you compare what you could gain from your work in the corporate world with the prospects of owning and operating your own business. You will compare both tangible and intangible dimensions.

Of all the factors that influence your decision of whether to go into business, the financial questions can be some of the most challenging. Some financial elements are less certain, especially at the beginning. And yet, when you are about to start a business, you have to take this uncertainty and somehow make your best guess as to how it will work out.

Applied to the decision of whether to quit your job and start a business, breakeven thinking becomes a comparison between what you could earn either way over a defined period of time.

The Formula

The breakeven formula used for this decision is a gross estimate based on many assumptions about market demand, the presence and actions of competitors in the market, the revenue stream of the business, the expense structure of the business, and all the assumptions related to keeping one's job. The formula is

$$BE = (R - [CA + CO]) + \Delta V = 0,$$

where

$$
\begin{aligned}
BE &= \text{Breakeven Point} \\
R &= \text{Revenue Expected From Starting the Company} \\
CA &= \text{Accounting Costs Expected to Be Incurred by} \\
  &\quad \text{Operating the Company} \\
CO &= \text{Opportunity Costs Expected to Be Incurred by} \\
  &\quad \text{Quitting Your Job} \\
\Delta V &= \text{Change in the Total Value of the Firm as a} \\
  &\quad \text{Result of Starting and Operating the Business.}
\end{aligned}
$$

If the result is a positive number (above the breakeven point of zero), then financially the decision makes sense. If the result is a negative number, then financially at least the decision would be unwise.

You will notice that two types of costs are included in this formula: accounting costs and opportunity costs. Accounting costs are the more familiar term. They will show up in the income statement. You can think of these as the operating expenses to run the company or the costs you incur to generate operating revenue. Opportunity costs are different. These are the economic costs from giving up what you might have earned by taking your next best alternative. In the case of deciding whether to quit your job and start a business, one opportunity cost is the after-tax wages and benefits you could have earned over a defined period of time by staying with your current job and not starting a business. These wages and benefits you will have to give up if you start a full-time business. Other opportunity costs include what you could earn from putting (or keeping) your cash in an investment other than starting a business—such as a money market account or your personal property. You incur these costs when you start a business and take your personal assets such as cash or give up your wage-earning job. These costs do not show up in the income statement, but they are (economic) costs.

Example

Consider Tally Richey, a 35-year-old woman, her husband Donovan, and their two young children. They live on 150 acres of land that contains three ponds and two running streams. Their business idea is to develop just half of the property into a golf course (nine holes) and small pro shop. The business would be a sole proprietorship. They plan to expand it to a full 18 holes a few years later as they build customer support and generate cash for landscape construction. They even have dreams of eventually buying the neighbor's property of 200 acres. Right now they have $100,000 of equity in their property, which they could refinance. Of this, $50,000 now sits in the family money market account that earns an annual percentage rate of 6%. They will have access to this cash when the money market instrument matures in 6 months. They plan to use this $50,000 to construct the landscape for the bare minimum needed to open the first nine holes. This will include one large putting green, nine tees, fairways and greens, and a driving range. They will also purchase two pieces of equipment for mowing—one for fairways and one for greens. Let's assume that since the business requires their full-time commitment, they will have to quit their jobs. In the business they will employ a few part-time workers.

Neither Tally nor Donovan has direct experience actually operating a public golf course. They have been avid golfers for 5 years and love the sport. They have a close circle of golfing-enthusiast friends, some of whom have spoken about the natural beauty of the Richey property and what a great golf course it could make. Clearly it is the asset of land and their passion for golf that might give Tally and Donovan a good start for their business idea.

Curious about whether the business would generate a profit, Tally asks a friend who is an accountant to prepare a projected income statement for the first 3 years of business operations. This they turn into a breakeven study, comparing their projections with what they could achieve by keeping their jobs.

Based on the information that Tally and Donovan gave the accountant, he brings them information given in Table D.1, Projected Breakeven Statement.

Sales projections are based on Tally and Donovan's estimates for the number of golfing customers paying a fixed amount for greens fees and other products. To begin with, the company will sell just a few items, such as a single line of golf clubs, putters, tees, and golf balls. Accounting costs include the costs of maintaining the nine-hole golf course, operating the tiny pro shop, and marketing. Tally and Donovan will pay themselves a wage for some of these expenses and can choose to take the rest

Table D.1. Projected Breakeven Statement

	Year 1	Year 2	Year 3	3-year total
Sales	$350,000	$500,000	$750,000	$1,600,000
Less cost of goods sold	$60,000	$80,000	$120,000	$260,000
Gross profit	$290,000	$420,000	$630,000	$1,340,000
Less accounting costs (operating expenses)	$210,000	$310,000	$470,000	$990,000
Net profit (before income taxes)	$80,000	$110,000	$160,000	$350,000
Less opportunity costs*	($166,000)	($172,000)	$178,000)	($516,000)
ΔV estimated change in the value of the firm**	$50,000	$50,000	$75,000	$155,000
Above (Below) breakeven	($36,000)	($12,000)	$57,000	$9,000

*Both Tally and Donovan giving up 3 years of salary and benefits plus the opportunity to invest $50,000 from the money market account, which now earns 6% interest.

**Considering the change in total value of the business (including the value of the developed property and what the business might be sold for at the end of the time period).

as a bonus at the end of the time period, or take the rest and invest it in growing the business.

Of course there are other options to consider for starting the business, which would make the financial projection results come out differently. For example, Tally could keep her job and Donovan could quit his job to oversee the landscape construction and opening of the business. Tally's job could provide the family with personal cash flow so they can keep making payments on their mortgage and living expenses. Assuming for sake of discussion that Tally and Donovan each earn roughly the same amount, Table D.2 presents a revised projected breakeven statement.

Summary

This type of breakeven study is a big-picture analysis. If Tally and Donovan can keep the business growing for 3 years and meet their assumptions, starting this business might be worth it. But this is a big IF! Nothing is guaranteed. Their assumptions about market demand, revenue, and expense structure may be unrealistic if they lack experience working at a golf course.

Table D.2. Revised Projected Breakeven Statement

	Year 1	Year 2	Year 3	3-year total
Sales	$350,000	$500,000	$750,000	$1,600,000
Less cost of goods sold	$60,000	$80,000	$120,000	$260,000
Gross profit	$290,000	$420,000	$630,000	$1,340,000
Less accounting costs (operating expenses)	$210,000	$310,000	$470,000	$990,000
Net profit (before income taxes)	$80,000	$110,000	$160,000	$350,000
Less opportunity costs*	($86,000)	($92,000)	($95,000)	($516,000)
ΔV estimated change in the value of the firm**	$50,000	$0,000	$75,000	$155,000
Above (Below) breakeven	$44,000	$68,000	$140,000	$252,000

*Donovan only giving up 3 years of salary and benefits plus the opportunity to invest $50,000 from the money market account, which now earns 6% interest.

**Considering the change in total value of the business (including the value of the developed property and what the business might be sold for at the end of the time period).

This application of breakeven analysis is not foolproof. Projecting the financial impact of one business idea compared with its best alternative (keeping your job) requires them to make their best reasonable *estimates*. Enthusiasm over an interesting business idea can cloud their judgment. Because financial projections are estimates based on assumptions that they make, Tally and Donovan may be tempted to do some interesting things with their estimates. For example, they may be tempted to under-represent opportunity costs. They may be aggressive with their assumptions regarding market demand, pricing, and sales. Or they may be less realistic regarding projected operating expenses.

APPENDIX E
Annuity Table

Years	4%	5%	6%	7%	8%	9%	10%	11%	
1	0.962	0.952	0.943	0.935	0.926	0.917	0.909	0.901	
2	1.886	1.859	1.833	1.808	1.783	1.759	1.736	1.713	
3	2.775	2.723	2.673	2.624	2.577	2.531	2.487	2.444	
4	3.630	3.546	3.465	3.387	3.312	3.240	3.170	3.102	
5	4.452	4.329	4.212	4.100	3.993	3.890	3.791	3.696	
6	5.242	5.076	4.917	4.767	4.623	4.486	4.355	4.231	
7	6.002	5.786	5.582	5.389	5.206	5.033	4.868	4.712	
8	6.733	6.463	6.210	5.971	5.747	5.535	5.335	5.146	
9	7.435	7.108	6.802	6.515	6.247	5.995	5.759	5.537	
10	8.111	7.722	7.360	7.024	6.710	6.418	6.145	5.889	
11	8.760	8.306	7.887	7.499	7.139	6.805	6.495	6.207	
12	9.385	8.863	8.384	7.943	7.536	7.161	6.814	6.492	
13	9.986	9.394	8.853	8.358	7.904	7.487	7.103	6.750	
14	10.563	9.899	9.295	8.745	8.244	7.786	7.367	6.982	
15	11.118	10.380	9.712	9.108	8.559	8.061	7.606	7.191	

Discount rate per year

Years	12%	13%	14%	15%	16%	17%	18%	19%	20%
1	0.893	0.885	0.877	0.870	0.862	0.855	0.847	0.840	0.833
2	1.690	1.668	1.647	1.626	1.605	1.585	1.566	1.547	1.528
3	2.402	2.361	2.322	2.283	2.246	2.210	2.174	2.140	2.106
4	3.037	2.974	2.914	2.855	2.798	2.743	2.690	2.639	2.589
5	3.605	3.517	3.433	3.352	3.274	3.199	3.127	3.058	2.991
6	4.111	3.998	3.889	3.784	3.685	3.589	3.498	3.410	3.326
7	4.564	4.423	4.288	4.160	4.039	3.922	3.812	3.706	3.605
8	4.968	4.799	4.639	4.487	4.344	4.207	4.078	3.954	3.837
9	5.328	5.132	4.946	4.772	4.607	4.451	4.303	4.163	4.031
10	5.650	5.426	5.216	5.019	4.833	4.659	4.494	4.339	4.192
11	5.938	5.687	5.453	5.234	5.029	4.836	4.656	4.486	4.327
12	6.194	5.918	5.660	5.421	5.197	4.988	4.793	4.611	4.439
13	6.424	6.122	5.842	5.583	5.342	5.118	4.910	4.715	4.533
14	6.628	6.302	6.002	5.724	5.468	5.229	5.008	4.802	4.611
15	6.811	6.462	6.142	5.847	5.575	5.324	5.092	4.876	4.675

Notes

Chapter 1

1. Bell (1969); Dean (1948); Earley (1955); Kempster (1949); Soldofsky (1959); Weiser (1969).

Chapter 2

1. Weygandt, Kimmel, and Kieso (2009).
2. Kempster (1949).

Chapter 4

1. Bell (1969), p. 34.

Chapter 5

1. Mariotti (2007).
2. See Gardner (1955).
3. Kimes and Thompson (2004).

Chapter 6

1. Kurtz (2008).
2. Pindyck and Rubinfeld (2001).
3. Pindyck and Rubinfeld (2001).
4. Mansfield, Allen, Doherty, and Weigelt (2002).
5. Mansfield, Allen, Doherty, and Weigelt (2002).
6. Mansfield, Allen, Doherty, and Weigelt (2002).
7. Kurtz (2008).
8. Smith and Nagle (1994).

Chapter 7

1. Hilton (2009), p. 290.

Chapter 8

1. Hilton (2009), p. 247.

Chapter 9

1. Hilton (2009), pp. 256–257.
2. Garrison, Noreen, and Brewer (2008), p. 203.
3. Hansen and Mowen (2007), p. 87.
4. Hansen and Mowen (2007), p. 87.

Chapter 10

1. Smith and Nagle (1994).
2. Tse (1960).

Chapter 11

1. Smith and Nagle (1994).
2. Tse (1960), p. 81.

Chapter 12

1. Hansen and Mowen (2007), pp. 536–537.

Chapter 14

1. For additional information on MACRS depreciation, the reader is directed to Hilton (2009), pp. 698–700.

2. For information on incorporating inflation into the analysis, the reader is directed to Hilton (2009), pp. 718–720.

3. Brealey, Myers, and Marcus (2008).

4. Guidry, Horrigan, and Craycraft (1998).

5. Brealey and Myers (2000).

6. Kempster (1949); Soldofsky (1959).

7. Cheung & Heaney (1990); Freeman and Freeman (1993); Guidry, Horrigan, and Craycraft (1998); Kee (2007).

8. Kinney and Raiborn (2008).

9. Brealey and Myers (2000), p. 27.

Chapter 15

1. Presented in Barnett and Ziegler (1991).
2. Barnett and Ziegler (1991).
3. Battista and Crowningshield (1966), pp. 14–15.
4. Brandenburger and Nalebuff (1996); Pindyck and Rubinfeld (2001), p. 23; Porter (1980), p. 167.

Chapter 16

1. Hilton (2009), pp. 304–306.

Appendix A

1. Magretta (2002); Schweizer (2005).
2. Bazerman (2006).
3. Garrison, Noreen, and Brewer (2008), pp. 201–202.
4. Garrison, Noreen, and Brewer (2008), p. 197.

Appendix B

1. Anderson (1957); Bell (1969); Chung (1993); Conway (1957); Fearon (1960); Freeman and Freeman (1993); Kee (2007); Schweitzer, Trossmann, and Lawson (1992); Soldofsky (1959); Weiser (1969); Yacobian (1959).
2. Garrison, Noreen, and Brewer (2008), p. 196.
3. Including Battista and Crowningshield (1966); Conway (1957); Dean (1948); Johnson (1965); Kempster (1949); Klipper (1978); Soldofsky (1959); Warthen (1972); and Yacobian (1959).
4. Dean (1948).
5. Schein (1996).
6. Senge (1990).
7. Child (2005); Maital (1994); Porter (1996); Prahalad and Hamel (1990).
8. Kempster (1949); Weiser (1969); Yacobian (1959).

Appendix C

1. Galbraith (1987), p. 172; Veblen (1904).
2. Compare with Kempster (1949), p. 712.
3. Hess (1897); Hess (1903).
4. National Association of Cost Accountants (1949).
5. Earley (1955).

6. Chatfield (1974).

7. McKinsey (1924).

8. Such as Dean (1948); Earley (1955); Kempster (1949); Tuttle (1959); and Weiner (1960).

9. Martin (1985).

10. Creese (1993).

11. Finch and Gavirneni (2006); Yunker (2001); Yunker (2006).

12. Gardner (1955); Schweitzer, Trossmann, and Lawson (1992); Tse (1960).

References

Anderson, C. W. (1957). Disclosure of assumptions key to better break-even analysis. *National Association of Accountants NAA Bulletin, 39*(4), 25–30.

Barnett, R. A., & Ziegler, M. R. (1991). *Essentials of college mathematics: For business, economics, life sciences and social sciences* (2nd ed.). New York: Dellen.

Battista, G. L., & Crowningshield, G. R. (1966). Cost behavior and breakeven analysis—a different approach. *National Association of Accountants NAA Management Accounting, 48*(2), 3–16.

Bazerman, M. H. (2006). *Judgment in managerial decision making* (6th ed.). New York: John Wiley & Sons.

Bell, A. L. (1969). Break-even charts versus marginal graphs. *Management Accounting, 59*(6), 32–35, 48.

Brandenburger, A. M., & Nalebuff, B. J. (1996). *Co-opetition.* New York: Doubleday.

Brealey, R. A., & Myers, S. C. (2000). *Principles of corporate finance* (6th ed.). Boston: Irwin McGraw-Hill.

Brealey, R. A., Myers, S. C., & Marcus, A. J. (2008). *Fundamentals of corporate finance* (6th ed.). New York: McGraw-Hill.

Chatfield, M. (1974). *A history of accounting thought.* Hinsdale, IL: The Dryden Press.

Cheung, J. K., & Heaney, J. (1990). A contingent-claim integration cost-volume-profit analysis with capital budgeting. *Contemporary Accounting Research, 6*(2), 738–760.

Child, J. (2005). *Organization: Contemporary principles and practice.* Malden, MA: Blackwell.

Chung, K. H. (1993). Cost-volume-profit analysis under uncertainty when the firm has production flexibility. *Journal of Business Finance & Accounting, 20*(4), 583–592.

Conway, R. W. (1957). Breaking out of the limitations of break-even analysis. *National Association of Cost Accountants NACA Bulletin, 38*(10), 1265–1272.

Creese, R. C. (1993). Break-even analysis—The fixed quantity approach. *Transactions of AACE International,* A.1, pp. A.1.1.–A.1.7.

Dean, J. (1948). Cost structures of enterprises and break-even charts. *The American Economic Review. Papers and Proceedings of the Sixtieth Annual Meeting of the American Economic Association, 38*(2), 153–164.

Earley, J. S. (1955). Recent developments in cost accounting and the "marginal analysis." *Journal of Political Economy, 63*(3), 227–242.

Fearon, H. E. (1960). Constant product mix a limiting assumption in B-E analysis. *National Association of Accountants NAA Bulletin, 41*(11), 61–67.

Finch, B., & Gavirneni, S. (2006). Confidence intervals for optimal selection among alternatives with stochastic variable costs. *International Journal of Production Research, 44*(20), 4329–4342.

Freeman, M., & Freeman, K. (1993). Considering the time value of money in breakeven analysis. *Management Accounting, 71*(1), 50–52.

Galbraith, J. K. (1987). *A history of economics.* London: Penguin Books.

Gardner, F. V. (1955). *Profit management and control.* New York: McGraw-Hill.

Garrison, R. H., Noreen, E. W., & Brewer, P. C. (2008). *Managerial accounting* (12th ed.). New York: McGraw-Hill Irwin.

Guidry, F., Horrigan, J. O., & Craycraft, C. (1998). CVP analysis: A new look. *Journal of Managerial Issues, 10*(1), 74–85.

Hansen, D. R., & Mowen, M. M. (2007). *Managerial accounting* (8th ed.). Mason, OH: Thomson South-Western.

Hess, H. (1897). Time saving and its relation to profits. *Engineering Magazine, 20*, 935 ff.

Hess, H. (1903). Manufacturing: Capital, costs, profits, and dividends. *Engineering Magazine, 24*, 367 ff.

Hilton, R. W. (2009). *Managerial accounting: Creating value in a dynamic business environment* (8th ed.). New York: McGraw-Hill Irwin.

Johnson, C. H. (1965). B-E analysis in cost control. *National Association of Accountants NAA Bulletin, 46*(8), 64.

Kee, R. (2007). Cost-volume-profit analysis incorporating the cost of capital. *Journal of Managerial Issues, 19*(4), 478–493.

Kempster, J. H. (1949). Break-even analysis—common ground for the economist and the cost accountant. *National Association of Cost Accountants NACA Bulletin, 39*(12), 711–720.

Kimes, S. E., & Thompson, G. M. (2004). Restaurant revenue management at Chevys: Determining the best table mix. *Decision Sciences, 35*(3), 371–392.

Kinney, M. R., & Raiborn, C. A. (2008). *Cost accounting: Foundations and evolutions* (7th ed.). Mason, OH: Cengage Learning.

Klipper, H. (1978). Breakeven analysis with variable product mix. *Management Accounting, 59*(10), 51–54.

Kurtz, D. L. (2008). *Contemporary marketing* (13th ed.). Mason, OH: Thomson South-Western.

Magretta, J. (2002). Why business models matter. *Harvard Business Review, 85*(5), 86–92.

Maital, S. (1994). *Executive economics.* New York: The Free Press.

Mansfield, E., Allen, W. B., Doherty, N. A., & Weigelt, K. (2002). *Managerial economics: Theory, applications, and cases* (5th ed.). New York: W. W. Norton.

Mariotti, S. (2007). *Entrepreneurship: Starting and operating a small business.* Upper Saddle River, NJ: Pearson Prentice Hall.

Martin, H. (1985). Breaking through the breakeven barriers. *Management Accounting, 66*(11), 31–34.

McKinsey, J. O. (1924). Co-ordination of sales, production, and finance. *The University Journal of Business, 2*(4), 399–405.

National Association of Cost Accountants. (1949). The analysis of cost-volume-profit relationships. *National Association of Cost Accountants NACA Bulletin, 31*(4), 523–564.

Pindyck, R. S., & Rubinfeld, D. L. (2001). *Microeconomics* (5th ed.). Upper Saddle River, NJ: Prentice Hall.

Porter, M. E. (1980). *Competitive strategy: Techniques for analyzing industries and competitors.* New York: The Free Press.

Porter, M. E. (1996). What is strategy? *Harvard Business Review, 74*(6), 61–78.

Prahalad, C. K., & Hamel, G. (1990). The core competence of the corporation. *Harvard Business Review, 68*(3), 79–91.

Schein, E. H. (1996). Three cultures of management: The key to organizational learning. *Sloan Management Review, 38*(1), 9–20.

Schweitzer, M., Trossmann, E., & Lawson, G. H. (1992). *Break-even analyses: Basic model, variants, extensions.* New York: John Wiley & Sons.

Schweizer, L. (2005). Concept and evolution of business models. *Journal of General Management, 31*(2), 37–56.

Senge, P. (1990). *The fifth discipline.* New York: Doubleday.

Smith, G. E., & Nagle, T. T. (1994). Financial analysis for profit-driven pricing. *Sloan Management Review, 35*(3), 71–84.

Soldofsky, R. M. (1959). Accountant's vs. economist's concepts of break-even analysis. *National Association of Cost Accountants NACA Bulletin, 41*(4), 5–18.

Tse, J. Y. D. (1960). *Profit planning through volume-cost analysis.* New York: Macmillan.

Tuttle, R. E. (1959). The effect of inventory change on break-even analysis. *National Association of Accountants NAA Bulletin, 40*(5), 77–87.

Veblen, T. (1904). *The theory of business enterprise.* New York: Charles Scribner's Sons.

Warthen, W. H. F., Jr. (1972). Mix variances in profit rate analysis. *Management Accounting, 53*(12), 43–45.

Weiner, J. (1960). To better results through a more accurate break-even formula. *National Association of Cost Accountants NACA Bulletin, 41*(11), 5–18.

Weiser, H. J. (1969). Break-even analysis: A re-evaluation. *Management Accounting, 50*(6), 36–41.

Weygandt, J. J., Kimmel, P. D., & Kieso, D. E. (2009). *Accounting principles* (9th ed.). New York: John Wiley & Sons.

Yacobian, P. (1959). A practical evaluation of breakeven analysis. *National Association of Accountants NAA Bulletin, 40*(5), 23–29.

Yunker, J. A. (2001). Stochastic CVP analysis with economic demand and cost functions. *Review of Quantitative Finance and Accounting, 17*(2), 127–149.

Yunker, J. A. (2006). Incorporating stochastic demand into breakeven analysis: A practical guide. *Engineering Economist, 51*(2), 161–193.

Further Reading

Baber, W. R., Ijiri, Y., & Kang, S. H. (1996). Profit-volume-exchange-rate analysis for planning international operations. *Journal of International Financial Management and Accounting, 7*(2), 85–101.

Bozarth, C. C., & Handfield, R. B. (2006). *Introduction to operations and supply chain management.* Upper Saddle River, NJ: Pearson Prentice Hall.

Bracken, R. M., & Volkan, A. G. (1988). Cash flow disclosures & break-even analysis. *The National Public Accountant, 33*(6), 48–51.

Conine, T. E., Jr. (1987). A pedagogical note on cash break-even analysis. *Journal of Business Finance & Accounting, 14*(3), 437–441.

Coppage, R. E., & Blum, L. M. (2007). Breakeven point analysis aids in evaluating ROTH conversions. *Practical Tax Strategies, 78*(2), 83–89.

Eckholdt, J. L. (1960). Using the break even chart in product-line decisions. *National Association of Accountants NAA Bulletin, 41*(11), 43–50.

Gapenski, L. C. (1989). Analysis provides test for profitability of new services. *Healthcare Financial Management, 43*(11), 48–58.

Gitman, L. J. (2000). *Principles of managerial finance.* Reading, MA: Addison-Wesley.

Harris, P. (1999). *Profit planning* (Hospitality Industry). (2nd ed.). Woburn, MA: Butterworth-Heinemann.

Heizer, J., & Render, B. (2001). *Operations management* (6th ed.). Upper Saddle River, NJ: Prentice Hall.

Kaplan, R. S., & Atkinson, A. A. (1989). *Advanced management accounting* (2nd ed.). Englewood Cliffs, NJ: Prentice Hall.

Kuratko, d. f., & Hodgetts, R. M. (2004). *Entrepreneurship: Theory, process, practice* (6th ed.). Mason, OH: Thomson South-Western.

Larimore, L. K. (1974). Break-even analysis for higher education. *Management Accounting, 56*(3), 25–28.

O'Neil, C. J., & Shackelford, D. A. (1989). An automobile lease-buy decision model. *Journal of Accountancy, 168*(3), 154–162.

Razek, J. R. (1989). Gain control of your organization's finances: Break-even analysis. *Nonprofit World, 7*(5), 30–33.

Render, B., & Stair, R. M., Jr. (1997). *Quantitative analysis for management* (6th ed.). Upper Saddle River, NJ: Prentice Hall.

Rigsbee, S. R., Ayaydin, S. S., & Richard, C. A. (1992). Secondary marketing: Pricing for profits. *Mortgage Banking, 52*(5), 65–71.

Sherman, L. F., Shim, J. K., & Hartney, M. (1993). Short run break-even analysis for real estate projects. *Real Estate Issues, 18*(1), 15–20.

Shim, J. K., & Constas, M. (1997). Does your nonprofit break even? *The CPA Journal, 67*(12), 36–42.

Suver, J. D., & Neumann, B. R. (1977). Patient mix and breakeven analysis. *Management Accounting, 58*(7), 38–40.

Willson, J. D. (1960). Practical applications of cost-volume-profit analysis. *National Association of Accountants NAA Bulletin, 41*(7), 5–19.

Index

various volumes, selling price (SP),
     85–87

W

weaknesses, net present value (NPV),
     100–102
weighted average cost of capital
     (WACC), 98
weighted averages, 45

in product mix, 41–49
     selling price (SP), 44, 45, 45*t*
     ticket price, 46*t*
weighted means, 126
Wellington, A. M., 132
Williams, John, 132

Z

Ziegler, M. R., 108

OTHER TITLES IN THE MANAGERIAL ACCOUNTING COLLECTION

Kenneth A. Merchant, University of Southern California, Collection Editor

- *The Small Business Controller* by Richard O. Hanson
- *Sustainability Reporting: Managing for Wealth and Corporate Health* by Gwendolen B. White
- *Business Planning and Entrepreneurship: An Accounting Approach* by Michael Kraten
- *Corporate Investment Decisions: Principles and Practice* by Michael Pogue
- *Drivers of Successful Controllership: Activities, People, and Connecting with Management* by Jurgen Weber and Pascal Nevries
- *Revenue Management: A Path to Increased Profits* by Ronald Huefner
- *Cost Management and Control in Government: Fighting the Cost War Through Leadership Driven Management* by Dale Geiger
- *Setting Performance Targets* by Carolyn Stringer and Paul Shantapriyan
- *Strategic Cost Analysis* by Roger Hussey and Audra Ong
- *Customer-Driven Budgeting Prepare, Engage, Execute: The Small Business Guide for Growth* by Floyd Talbot
- *Economic Decision Making Using Cost Data: A Guide for Managers* by Daniel M. Marburger and Ryan Peterson
- *Revenue Management in Service Organizations* by Paul Rouse, William McGuire, and Julie Harrison
- *Value Creation in Management Accounting: Using Information to Capture Customer Value* by CJ McNair-Connolly, Lidija Polutnik, Riccardo Silvi, and Ted Watts

Announcing the Business Expert Press Digital Library

Concise E-books Business Students Need
for Classroom and Research

This book can also be purchased in an e-book collection by your library as
- a one-time purchase,
- that is owned forever,
- allows for simultaneous readers,
- has no restrictions on printing, and
- can be downloaded as PDFs from within the library community.

Our digital library collections are a great solution to beat the rising cost of textbooks. E-books can be loaded into their course management systems or onto students' e-book readers.

The **Business Expert Press** digital libraries are very affordable, with no obligation to buy in future years. For more information, please visit **www.businessexpertpress.com/librarians**. To set up a trial in the United States, please email **sales@businessexpertpress.com**.

CPSIA information can be obtained
at www.ICGtesting.com
Printed in the USA
BVHW061753020321
601442BV00011B/425